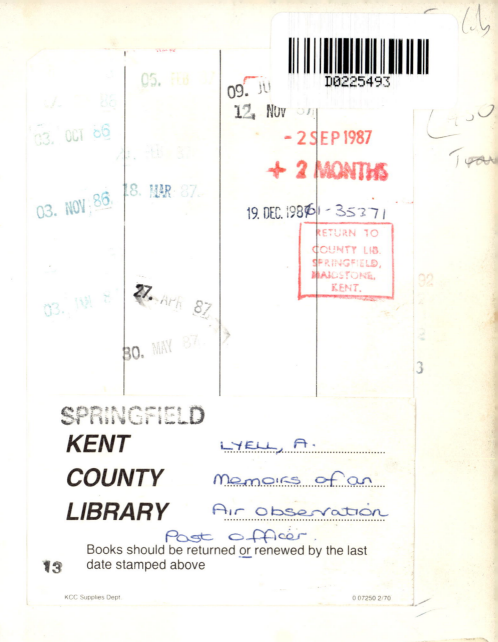

MEMOIRS OF
AN AIR OBSERVATION
POST OFFICER

The Author, September 1939.

MEMOIRS OF AN AIR OBSERVATION POST OFFICER

MAJOR ANDREW LYELL,
DFC, Croix de Guerre, RA

Contents

.

Photoset in AM International Plantin
Text paper supplied by Howard Smith Papers, Bristol
Printed in Great Britain by Picton Print
Citadel Works, Bath Road, Chippenham, Wilts
PP50755

EXPLANATION OF TERMS USED IN THE BOOK

AGRA — A grouping of artillery regiments of varying type and number forming a reserve of fire power in the hands of the Army Commander.

Air OP — Air Observation Post. A light aeroplane, then an Auster, flown by Royal Artillery pilots primarily for the observation of fire.

Air OP Squadron — A Royal Air Force Unit consisting of SHQ (Squadron Headquarters) and three Flights ('A', 'B' and 'C' Flights) attached to the Royal Artillery of a Corps.

Army Air OP Squadron — An Air OP Squadron forming a reserve of Air OP in the hands of the Army Commander. In fairly static warfare each Flight normally supported an AGRA, but in mobile warfare the Flights were sent by the Army Commander wherever they were needed.

ALG — Advanced Landing Ground. In practice an ALG was any field used only by Air OP aircraft.

BRA — Brigadier, Royal Artillery. The artillery adviser to an Army Commander.

CCRA — Corps Commander, Royal Artillery. The Artillery Brigadier at a Corps Headquarters commanding the Artillery of a Corps.

CRA — Commander, Royal Artillery. The Artillery Brigadier at a Divisional Headquarters or at an AGRA Headquarters commanding the Divisional Artillery or the AGRA.

Tac Army — The Tactical Headquarters of the Army Commander, General Sir Miles Dempsey, KCB, KBE, DSO, MC, which was habitually located not far behind the Army's front line. Here the Army Commander was assisted by a few chosen junior staff officers under Major Robert Priestley and by his two ADCs Capt Henry Whitworth and Captain 'Dickie' Dawson. He was protected by his own Bodyguard.

CBO — Counter Battery Officer at Corps who was in charge of the task of using our artillery to knock out the enemy's artillery.

FDLs — Forwarded Defended Localities, ie the front line.

HT cables — High Tension Cables.

Main Army — The Main Army Headquarters which was much further back from the front line. The Chief of Staff and the BRA were to be found here with all the other Army Staff Officers concerned with operations.

Rear Army	The Rear Army Headquarters was far behind the front line, and here were to be found all the staff who were not actively concerned with operations.
Tac 21 Army Group	The Tactical Headquarters of Field Marshal Lord Montgomery.
Mike Target	A target fired on by a Regiment of Artillery.
Victor Target	A target fired on by a Divisional Artillery.
Yoke Target	A target fired on by an AGRA.
ML Target	A target fired on by an even larger concentration of Artillery.
Scale 4	Each gun of the concentration of guns was to fire four rounds and then stop.
CGI	Chief Ground Instructor, responsible for the teaching at 43 OTU (Officers' Training Unit) of all Air OP subjects other than flying instruction.
CFI	Chief Flying Instructor.
GII	Short for GSO II (General Service Officer, ie Staff Officer). A GI was a Lt-Colonel; a GII a Major, and a GIII a Captain.

CHAPTER I
Prologue

On the 3rd of September 1939, war was declared between Great Britain and Germany. This should not have been a surprise to anyone but in fact most people had clung to the optimistic belief that another world war was so unthinkable that it would somehow be avoided. Unfortunately Hitler had attached too much importance to the relative military weakness of Britain and France and to the vote of the Oxford University Union that its members would not fight for King and Country. He was convinced that he could get whatever he wanted without another war. During the period of the 'Phoney War', which ended so abruptly in May 1940, we still hoped that sanity would eventually prevail and that since we obviously could not drive the German troops out of Poland, peace would soon be made. I knew very little about the Stock Exchange in those days but I remember being told that they were convinced that the war would be over by Christmas 1939.

Two days before the declaration of war I decided that the time had come for me to 'join up'. The question for me was what I should join. During my three years at Cambridge University I had been in the Cambridge University Artillery during the first year in 1930/31. The guns were still pulled by horses in those days and at our annual camp at Larkhill I much enjoyed riding one of the four horses that pulled each gun about Salisbury Plain.

During my second year at Cambridge I was in the University Cavalry Squadron. It was enormous fun learning such games as tent-pegging, cavalry drill and charging with drawn swords. That year the Government decided to save money by cancelling our annual camp and in lieu thereof we were attached to the Queen's Bays at Shorncliffe for fourteen days. During my third year I was in the University Infantry as I had formed the opinion that cavalry would never be used in war again.

During both my second and third years at Cambridge I had also been in the University Air Squadron. We flew from nearby Duxford where there was then an operational squadron of Bristol Bulldog fighters, though we learned on the Avro 504 and then graduated to the Atlas which I think had been used as a fighter towards the end of the First World War. The Avro was an extremely safe aircraft but the Atlas was a bit dangerous and one of us was killed in an Atlas at my first annual camp at Netheravon.

Our lecture rooms were filled with large coloured posters, designed in the previous war, teaching us elementary principles such as 'Beware of the Hun in the Sun'. The flight sergeant who instructed us in engines was so anxious that we should all pass the annual exam that he advised us to make a detailed copy of an engine inside a packet of Du Maurier cigarettes just in case we should need to refresh our memories during the exam. He himself supervised the actual exam.

We of course all wore parachutes when flying and on more than one occasion a parachute opened accidentally on the ground, possibly in the slipstream of an aircraft which was being

1

On the 5th of June 1985, the Author returned to Netheravon, in Wiltshire, and was entertained by Major Nick Parker, Officer Commanding 658 Squadron.

run up. This so infuriated the parachute packer at Duxford that he wired up our parachutes so that they would not open. Unfortunately for the packer this was discovered one day by an inspector of parachutes and there was the most frightful row.

It never happened to me, but there were occasions at that time when after an overhaul an aircraft was put together wrongly so that the ailerons operated in reverse. So we were taught always to check that the ailerons were working correctly before take-off.

Flying in those days was a bit different to Air OP flying. Climbing turns were strictly forbidden after take-off until we had attained a safe height in case the aircraft should go into a spin. All landings were by gliding approach: the throttle was not to be used at all unless it should be necessary to go round again. Aerobatics were very important and these included the 'falling leaf' which in subsequent years became obsolete as later aircraft would only have gone into a spin. We had no instruction in landings in fields as all landings in the prescribed 'forced landing field' had to be by gliding approach.

At Netheravon during our annual camp I was sent on a long cross-country flight. By the time I returned, the wind had swung round to the opposite direction. When landing I omitted to check the windsock and so landed downwind which one certainly should not do in an Avro. After touching down, my aircraft would not stop (there were no brakes in those days and so I could not turn), bounced across a road and ended up in a stubble field. The tail skid was broken and I got a rocket.

I see in my log book that I was graded 'above average'. Such a grading for a beginner became very rare during the Second World War as it was found to encourage pilots to become too confident and to kill themselves as a result.

After leaving Cambridge in the summer of 1933, I was attached for ten weeks to the 2nd Battalion The Black Watch at Colchester, my idea then being to become an infanteer in a Highland regiment. My platoon commander was Bernard Fergusson who later, when a brigadier, distinguished himself in Burma during the War. He wore a monocle and no one dared to ask him whether it was necessary or whether he only wore it because it made him look so fierce. I think I owed much to the early training which I received from him. I have referred to him by name because he was a very remarkable man. Though he was, at the time when I was under him for instruction, still only a second lieutenant, I regarded him with all the respect and deference as if he had been at least a captain. He was tall, distinguished-looking and an absolute professional at his job. He was obviously destined for great things. In fact he joined the Wingate expedition into Burma in 1943–44, and commanded the 16th Infantry Brigade in the 1944 expedition. He became Governor-General and C-in-C of New Zealand 1962–67. In 1972 he was created Baron (Life Peer) Ballantrae, KT, GCMG, GCVO, DSO. He died in November 1980.

At that time a Highland regiment would not accept an officer unless he had a private income of at least £500 a year – £1,200 a year was essential for the cavalry and the figure for the Household Cavalry was even higher still. This was because it was believed that certain standards must be maintained and because the pay of Army officers was appallingly low, I think an Army private was then paid only about two shillings a day but I never had personal experience of serving in the ranks.

It did not seem to me to be a good time to embark on a career in the Army. None of the officers thought that there would be another world war and peacetime soldiering seemed deadly dull. There was individual training, then company training, then battalion training and finally brigade training. But there were many days on which there was nothing for me to do after 'Company Office' at 1000 hrs at which either the Company Commander or Bernard Fergusson delivered devastating rockets and some punishments to offenders. So I spent a great deal of time playing the bagpipes under the tuition of the Corporal Piper. I remember getting into trouble for playing the 'Flowers of the Forest' on the bagpipes: except on funereal occasions it had to be practised only on the chanter. I also got into trouble when my deerhound somehow escaped from my bedroom and treed the garrison cat on the parade ground during a battalion parade.

Promotion in the Army was at that time far too slow. There was one subaltern who had won the MC during the First World War and yet still had to take his turn as orderly officer. So I decided that the Army was not for me. I became a barrister instead.

CHAPTER II
The Queen's Own Dorset Yeomanry

At the end of August 1939, I was staying with an aunt who lived at Queen Camel, near Sherborne and beginning to get my horse fit for hunting during the coming season with the Blackmore Vale. War was then imminent and I felt that I had to join something before it began. Ever since my attachment to The Black Watch I had remained an officer in the Territorial Army Reserve of Officers. And, by reason of my time in the Cambridge University Air Squadron, I could reasonably have hoped to be accepted by the Royal Air Force. My first choice would have been to become a fighter pilot, but at my then age of 27 I might have been ordered to fly bombers and it was unthinkable that I might have to drop bombs on a Germany in which a certain very important girl friend of mine might be living. So I joined the Dorset Yeomanry the day before war was declared and went with the Sherborne battery to Shaftesbury where we joined the Dorchester battery.

In my aunt's house in Queen Camel there was a copy of the celebrated painting by Elizabeth Butler of the Charge of the Dorset Yeomanry at Agadir. I think they were charging a tribe named the Senussi. The faces of the actual officers who took part in this charge were accurately depicted in this picture. Among these were Freddie Digby who was then commanding the Regiment and who was, in 1939, its Colonel. He was the Master of the Blackmore Vale Foxhounds and lived at Sherborne Castle. I knew him and his family fairly well and liked them a lot. The Commanding Officer was Henry Mitchell who had been, before his retirement to our hunting country, a commander in the Royal Navy. Some of his ideas as to drill were somewhat 'Senior Service' – everything was to be done at the double. The adjutant was Bunny Huddlestone, a retired gunner officer who had become hunt secretary of the Blackmore Vale. I knew them as Henry and Bunny respectively but after I had joined the Regiment I realized that I could no longer call them by their christian names. It was not long before Henry was recalled to the Navy and Bunny was sent to command a regular battery in France. After that we were for a time a regiment of complete amateurs.

The officers were billeted in the Grosvenor Hotel at Shaftesbury where we were reasonably comfortable. It was an ancient building in which the bedrooms were on a lower level than the passage outside them. As a result one opened one's bedroom door and then was apt to fall down the three steps into the bedroom. I shared a room with a friend who had been with me at Marlborough: he had a radio and so we had the doubtful pleasure before we went to sleep of hearing Lord Haw-Haw announce which ships of our Navy had been sunk each day. That was a time when only the Royal Navy was actively engaged in the War.

All the empty houses in Shaftesbury were requisitioned for the men. Palliasses (sacks filled with straw) were not yet available and each man had to make do with only three Army blankets. Each room of each requisitioned house had to contain as many men as it would hold and some of the rooms had stone floors. As there was no heating, some of these stone floors remained damp for a considerable time after they had been scrubbed. I felt somewhat ashamed at having to ask the men of my troop to put up with such discomfort. I would have

4

liked to have invited them to fetch mattresses and further blankets from their own homes nearby but my views were not shared by Higher Authority. I then resolved that, if ever I had a command of my own, no one under me would ever be more uncomfortable than was absolutely necessary. Extreme discomfort is surely not a necessary part of training for war.

The Regiment had long since ceased to be cavalry and become artillery. It was equipped with a total of four 18-pounder guns which were relics of the previous war. I don't think we had any ammunition. The guns were kept in a field on the outskirts of Shaftesbury which was reserved for the purposes of our training. We had practically no vehicles until I was sent with a party of drivers by train to Southampton to fetch a considerable number of ancient and broken down motor cars which the Army had acquired. I use the words 'broken down' because most of them either broke down or ran out of petrol on the way back to Shaftesbury. This was my responsibility and it was fortunate for me that I had a number of men with me who had been excellent mechanics in civilian life or we would never have got all those cars to Shaftesbury. The finest of all these mechanics had been Lord Digby's chauffeur: in those days a chauffeur of his standing could not only decarbonize a car but also rebore it.

In addition to the guard which had of course to be mounted on the gun park, there was a PAD (Passive Air Defence) Squad which had to be continuously in readiness in case Shaftesbury were suddenly to be blitzed by enemy aircraft. Their job was to put out fires and deal with gas attacks, though they had had no training in either task. I wondered who thought up this extraordinary idea. Not even London had been bombed at that time and none of us had even seen an enemy aircraft. Yet a considerable body of men under a sergeant had to be in readiness all night wearing tin hats, battle dress with gas masks and anti-gas capes, boots and gaiters and in a small room which, by reason of the fact that the blackout boards had to be in position thereby preventing the entrance of any fresh air, was filled with cigarette smoke and germs from those who had streaming colds. It must have been hell for them. After some weeks of this, one night when I was orderly officer I decided that it was time that something was done about this PAD Squad. So I wrote a very strong and scathing report on it and submitted this to the acting commanding officer. I expected to receive a severe rocket, but in fact the PAD Squad was thereupon disbanded.

I am not going to criticize this territorial acting CO: he had no real military experience and he was doing his best. But he did make some mistakes. One night he decided to turn out the guard in the early hours of the morning. He found the sentry correctly on duty but the guard commander and the rest of the guard were sound asleep in the guard room. So he helped himself to all their rifles and took these back to his hotel bedroom. I think he later realized that what he had done was not the correct procedure in those circumstances. At any rate no further disciplinary action was taken.

As I had been an infantry officer, one thing that I could do was drill my troop. When they were expert at all the movements set out in the drill book, this became rather tedious. So I started a practice of calling out each man in turn and telling him to take over my job as troop commander while I took his place in the ranks. In this way I found out which of the men were suitable for promotion or to be sent for training as officers. One day I told the troop that the Queen was about to inspect them. Then I called out two of the men, one to be the troop commander and the other, the troop humorist, to be 'the Queen'. I took my place in the ranks and then saw that the CO had arrived unexpectedly on the drill ground and was standing watching us. I pretended not to notice and allowed the comedy to continue. 'The Queen' was magnificent. 'She' spoke to each of the men, questioning him as to where he came from, what he had done in civilian life and what he thought of life in the Army.

5

The Dorset Yeomen were a superb body of men. Most of them came from the farming community and they had the sound commonsense of countrymen. They were unflappable in an emergency and as a result they were not soldiers who would be likely ever to panic. They had a tremendous sense of humour. They were always loyal to me and did their very best on any special occasion such as an exercise. An officer is judged by the performance of the men under him: my 'E' Troop never failed me. I know that they referred to themselves as 'Uncle Andy's Boys' though I was only 27. I remember those men with affection and gratitude. Whenever I meet a man who says 'I said to I', etc I know that he comes from Dorset.

My Sergeant i/c Signals was named Murphy and as his name suggests, was an Irishman though his home was in Sherborne. He was quite brilliant at his job: all my telephone lines were invariably laid long before those of any other troop and I never had any worries through wireless sets failing. But Irishmen can be very difficult to handle and Sgt Murphy was no exception: perhaps his brilliance made him temperamental. My Troop Sgt-Major on quite a number of occasions came to me to complain of Sgt Murphy's insubordination and to demand that he be put on some serious charge. The men of Dorset could also be difficult to handle and I spent many hours arguing with and persuading these two men to reconcile their differences. I was certainly not going to put any man as outstanding as Murphy on any charge unless I had absolutely no alternative.

Sgt Murphy persistently refused to have his name put forward as a candidate for a commission but after I had left the Dorset Yeomanry and gone to the Air OP, he eventually agreed to this. I understand that he ended the War as a major and instructor of gunnery at Larkhill. Many years after the War I heard that he was managing director of a successful company somewhere in the Midlands.

Every man had to be taught to drive the vehicles both by day and by night. The headlamps and even the sidelights had to be blacked out in conformity with blackout regulations. My subsequent flying experience convinced me that those regulations when enforced in the countryside were quite absurd and did far more harm than good. It is somewhat alarming to teach a driver under instruction to drive a truck with only sidelights which had been partially blacked out around narrow Dorset lanes on a dark and misty night.

We were now the 141 Field Regiment RA but during this period of the 'Phoney War' we still behaved in many ways as if we were still the Dorset Yeomanry. Officers wore the special Dorset Yeomanry hats with green bands round them, our distinctive lanyards, also riding breeches with canary-coloured strappings and highly-polished gunner riding boots. We even wore spurs during the first week or so of the War. Michael Stancomb and I borrowed two loose boxes from friends in Shaftesbury and fetched our horses there where our batmen acted as our grooms – as well as being our official drivers as provided by the establishment. Both batmen had been grooms before the War and were delighted to have this job. We hunted every Saturday with the Blackmore Vale and in the early spring of 1940, when the Regiment was stationed at Frome, we hunted with the Beaufort. The Duke was himself hunting his hounds and we, as serving officers in uniform, were not asked to pay any 'cap'. We both rode in the 43 Div point-to-point which was organized by the South and West Wilts Hunt. We trained our horses for this race by early morning gallops in Longleat Park – where the lions are now.

At my suggestion the Regiment, when at Frome, held a night exercise at Heaven's Gate in Longleat Park. All the stars were shining brightly that night and the setting could scarcely have been more beautiful. A visiting IG (Instructor of Gunnery) decided to check every gun so as to ensure that all guns were correctly layed and parallel. So he asked that each gun be ordered to take a bearing on the left star in Orion's Belt. He did not order synchronization of watches or that the bearing should be taken at any precise time. He began to be somewhat critical of the result but it was then pointed out to him that Orion moves in the sky as the Earth rotates. Incidentally my experience throughout the War was that if one selects an exceptionally beautiful spot for an exercise, an inspecting general or brigadier will be influenced by the environment and that this will be likely to modify any criticism which he might otherwise have made. For this reason, when I was later commanding my Air OP Squadron at Old Sarum, I used to select the lovely village of Crawley as the location of my SHQ in any exercise which was being watched by any very senior officer.

In January 1940, I was sent on a gas course at Winterbourne Gunner. There we learned all about every weapon of war which depended on the use of poison gas. But the most unpleasant part of this course was when we all had to enter a gas chamber. First there was a test which was designed to give us confidence in the efficiency of our gas masks. This involved our putting on our gas masks and spending two minutes in the chamber filled with the deadly chlorine gas – which incidentally smells like new-mown hay. We were laughingly told that anyone whose gas mask leaked would die. None of us in fact did die.

The next test was designed to give us experience of DM gas which makes one feel like death for the rest of the day, merely bloody awful during the following day and totally unable to tolerate cigarette smoke for the following week. The fear was that the Germans might use it against us just before they attacked. If they were to do so, our Army would be quite unable to resist their attack. Anyone who has ever experienced DM gas can recognise it immediately during the rest of his life, whereas other troops would not know that it was in the air until it was too late. So we as gas officers had to be poisoned by the wretched stuff so that in battle we would be able to give immediate warning to everyone to put on their gas masks.

Unfortunately the time selected for this ordeal was a Friday afternoon and many of us, including me, had dates with our girl friends in London that evening. Most people can hold their breath for about a minute and so it was arranged that we should all remain in the gas chamber without gas masks for two minutes. I now wish that I had given up smoking forever after that ordeal.

After that course I was given a 'distinguished' classification which did me no harm at all with my CO, but I suspect that this was not due entirely to my performance in the written exam but partly to the fact that I was one of the volunteers who wore for several days around their necks a thing which was designed to disclose immediately any traces of mustard gas which might be dropped by an enemy aircraft. Real mustard gas was fortunately not used for this test.

One sentence uttered by a lecturer on the subject of decontamination raised a laugh: 'If wooden furniture has been contaminated by mustard gas you should act as follows – if it is government furniture, burn it, but if it is your own furniture then, etc.' This distinction between government property and one's own property is surely still relevant today.

When I returned to the Regiment I found that no one was in the least interested in learning about gas. I was asked to give one gas lecture to the Regiment but after that the subject was forgotten. We all quite rightly believed that gas would never be used in this War because both sides had it and it was very unpleasant stuff. Of course if the Germans alone had had it and had been aware of our lack of it, Hitler would probably have ordered its use at a late stage in the War when things became desperate for him. This thought should help us to understand the value of our retaining a nuclear deterrent.

While we were still at Shaftesbury our territorial acting commanding officer was posted

7

away and we got a regular in his place. He was not a success. We saw very little of him as he took up residence in a different hotel to the rest of us and kept very much to himself. But on his formal Saturday morning inspections he always appeared to be very angry and totally devoid of any sense of humour. In fact we were all a bit terrified of him.

One evening he suddenly informed my then territorial battery commander that he would inspect our battery PAD Squad at 1100 hrs the following morning. This order caused considerable consternation as we hadn't a PAD Squad and I was really the only person who knew anything about gas. I was, therefore, ordered to have a fully-trained PAD Squad on parade at 1100 hrs the following morning in the Tanyard at Frome.

I said that I must have a sergeant to take charge of this squad. As it looked as if this job might become one of indefinite duration, no one was willing to offer any sergeant. Then Michael Stancomb, the battery captain, said that there was a sergeant cook who was not only a bad cook but also very dirty. We had inherited this sergeant cook from the Regiment's Territorial Army days and Michael was most anxious to get rid of him, but the fact that he was a sergeant and not fit for any other job provided a problem. So this dirty sergeant cook became abruptly the sergeant in charge of the PAD Squad.

Then I still needed at least four other ranks. There was a delightful man in my troop who had been on a civilian gas course just before he joined up. He was clearly the man to answer all the Colonel's questions and thereby save the situation. In addition to these two candidates for my instruction in gas I was allotted three men of very low mentality. These men were clearly not wanted by their troop commanders because they were quite unable to obey, or even comprehend, any orders: on any exercise that was important the usual procedure was to hide such men in the cookhouse. That was before the time when the procedure was adopted to send such men to see a psychiatrist (we called them 'trick cyclists') who would arrange for them to be transferred to a Pioneer battalion or released from the Army altogether.

I really did try that evening to teach these men all about gas, decontamination and anti-gas clothing. I think the sergeant learned quite a lot, the man in my troop knew most of it already and the other three failed to comprehend anything. So before the parade the following morning I dressed the three not so bright ones in anti-gas clothing complete with their gas masks on. I decided that the other two should be similarly dressed but should not be wearing their gas masks so that they would be able to answer any questions which the Colonel might put to them. I correctly guessed that the Colonel would not ask the sergeant any questions as he would imagine that the sergeant would know all the answers. I foolishly thought that in this way I had ensured that only the intelligent member of my troop would be asked any questions. I, of course, checked that each man had the correct quantity of eye shields and decontamination cream in his gas mask.

That inspection was for me a disaster. The Colonel stopped in front of the least intelligent man who was wearing a gas mask and told him that he had just been sprayed with mustard gas and that he was to take off all the anti-gas clothing. When, after very considerable difficulty, the man had succeeded in doing so, the Colonel gave him a severe rocket for having got all the mustard gas on to his face and hands and battledress. Then the Colonel told the sergeant to show him what he had in his gas mask case. The sergeant produced his gas mask, two eyeshields and the anti-gas cream, but the Colonel insisted on the case being completely emptied. To my horror out came knife, fork and spoon, a dirty old pair of socks and other things which certainly should not have been there.

At about this time our battery was inspected by the divisional commander of 43 Div. We took enormous trouble to ensure that nothing went wrong. But unfortunately the only access to the guardroom, which was beside the gate into the Tanyard at Frome, was by a step ladder. When the General arrived at the gate the sentry shouted 'Turn out the Guard', and the guard followed each other down that step ladder a bit too fast. The last man tripped and fell, bringing the others with him so that they all landed in a heap at the General's feet.

Not long after this our unpopular Colonel was posted to Burma. It was whispered that strings had been pulled in very high places to get rid of him after he had called a guard commander a 'bloody bastard' in the presence of his guard. It was not considered permissible for anyone to abuse a Dorset Yeoman in this manner. Just before this event we had posted to us two regulars as battery commanders and a regular adjutant. Our new Colonel, Woodward, won not only our admiration but also our affection. He took the trouble to get to know us all personally and he used to give all the officers talks which included references to his own experiences during the previous war. Lt-Col Woodward later became a brigadier: he certainly, in my opinion, deserved to become a general.

These new appointments led to the Regiment ceasing to be amateurs and becoming real professionals ready to go to war.

My new battery commander, Roscoe Turner, was a martinet, but this was precisely what we needed. I liked him a lot. As I never heard that he had become a general, I assumed that he had been killed during the War. I have heard that Ginger Bidwell, who became our adjutant, did survive the War.

One sunny day in 1940 when we were at St Albans we were on an extremely exhausting battery exercise and were hot, sweaty and tired. The men were obviously fed up and so I obtained permission from Roscoe to call for volunteers for a 'decontamination exercise'. There was some hesitation among the men who disliked the idea of wearing anti-gas clothing in that heat. But about twenty-five men, mostly from my own troop, volunteered, and I bundled them all into a 3-ton lorry and took them to the luxurious Harpenden swimming pool. The management admitted us on my paying the usual entrance fee for each man and I bought them each a pint of beer. Underpants served as swimming trunks. Some of the few local residents who were at the swimming pool may have disapproved but we all enjoyed ourselves immensely. After that I never had any difficulty in obtaining volunteers.

In the early weeks of the War an order had come down from the War Office that every officer must learn to ride a motorcycle and that brigadiers must be prepared to ride pillion. Presumably it was assumed that brigadiers would be too old to learn to ride motorcycles otherwise than as passengers.

When we were at St Albans, the Colonel decreed that there should be a motorcycle cross-country test for all officers. It was to be largely across country but the course included a number of minor lanes, a ford in which several of us came to grief and a long straight stretch of major road on which we all went as fast as the Army motorcycles were capable of going – which was over 75 mph. I think the Colonel intended the test to be like a modern rally but of course we regarded it as a race. Fortunately no one was seriously hurt.

9

CHAPTER III

The Real War Begins

Up to the time when the German Army broke through the lines of the Allies early in May 1940, many of us still hoped that peace would be made and no real war would ever begin. As soon as the real war did begin, 43 Div, of which we formed part, was ordered to move from Somerset to the area of St Albans.

All signposts had long since been removed from the roads of England as it was believed that they might assist German troops. In my days with the Cambridge University Air Squadron the drill if one should become lost was to fly low next to a railway station and read its name from the station board but these boards were also removed during the War. All race-courses, unused airfields and any open ground where German gliders might have landed were now covered with ancient vehicles which were so close together that later even the Air OP would think twice before landing there.

So I was allotted a motorcycle for myself and twenty-two military police who were also on motorcycles and sent off ahead of the Division with orders to leave one of the MPs to direct the vehicles of the Division at each place where these vehicles might otherwise have taken a wrong turning. My problem was that I must not run out of MPs before the prescribed route reached St Albans. It was believed that no vehicle would require refuelling on the way but there was a refuelling point for use in an emergency a little way down a side road not far from our destination.

After performing my task I waited by the roadside to watch all the vehicles of the Division go by, fervently hoping that none of them had got lost. None of them had done so, except the vehicles and guns of our Dorchester battery who had decided to refuel at the refuelling point and had then got lost when trying to find their way back to the prescribed route.

The Dorchester battery commander was furious with me for what had happened and criticized me severely that evening in the Mess. I defended myself, perhaps in too forthright a manner, and as a result my own battery commander ordered me to apologize to the indignant major, which I of course did in the appropriate formal manner. One should never answer back when criticized by a senior officer. However, Col Woodward somehow heard what had happened, sent for me and congratulated me on having done an excellent job and said that 'only a bloody fool would have got lost'. It was shortly after that that I was promoted to the rank of captain.

After the fall of France and during the evacuation from Dunkirk, the Regiment was sent from St Albans to camp in the open in Hatfield Forest. From there we watched the night sky which clearly showed the terrible bombing of London every night.

I had become the regimental mess secretary which meant that I had to run the Officers' Mess, keep the accounts, collect cheques at the end of each month and pay all the bills. After we had arrived in Hatfield Forest I, as usual, collected the officers' cheques and posted them to the Westminster Bank at St Albans. Then I dealt with all the bills and posted cheques to all our creditors at St Albans. I, as usual, paid the cheques into the bank a day or two before I paid the bills so that the balance at credit in the bank should be adequate to meet the bills. But, by reason of the bombing which I had watched, London was in a state of chaos and so was the postal service which went via London. As a result the cheques to the bank arrived a day after the cheque to a certain large shop in St Albans. The cheque to the shop was presented to the bank immediately on arrival and the bank on the same day returned it to the shop marked 'R.D.' Whereupon the shop immediately wrote an insulting letter to our Colonel protesting that we had failed to pay this debt.

The Colonel sent for me and I explained the situation to him. He knew that letters took at least ten days to pass through London. He was as angry as I was and told me to take a motor-cycle and to go straight back to St Albans, tell the bank what I thought of them, pay the shop's bill and tell them that if ever we went back to St Albans (which we in fact did) we would never deal with them again. This I much enjoyed doing.

We were then expecting an imminent invasion of our country by a German Army and we all intended to fight to the death. It never occurred to any of us that we would ever surrender. Churchill was voicing the thoughts of us all when he made his famous speech, 'We will fight on the beaches . . . we will never surrender.' And this bloody shop was worrying about its money.

After a month or two in Hatfield Forest the Regiment was ordered back to St Albans. We then received from on high orders which I now regard as a bit hysterical. For example, I was ordered to visit every petrol station in that district so that I might thereafter be prepared to blow them all up immediately the Germans landed. I was not a sapper and I still do not know how to blow up a petrol station. And what if the petrol might subsequently be required for our own troops? We assumed that this order came from someone at the War Office.

A Col Hilton came to lecture all the gunner officers of the Division. He told us that a Charles Bazeley, a gunner officer who had been seconded to the Royal Air Force some years before for army co-operation flying, was about to train a number of gunner officers to fly light unarmed aircraft which would operate from fields just behind the Army's front line. In this way the gunner officers could be briefed on the spot to seek targets and to observe the fire of the guns. In view of what had happened to the Lysander aircraft just about all of which had been shot down in the fighting which culminated in the fall of France, we considered that the life of an Air OP pilot would be exciting but short. In fact Charles Bazeley and Eric Joyce had had light unarmed aircraft in France but as soon as the retreat began they were ordered to fly back to England. Had they not done so there would have been no Air OP.

I volunteered immediately. I was convinced that I would soon be killed and the Air OP would provide me with a most exciting death.

From that time we had battery or regimental exercises every day and some of these exercises lasted several days. We were becoming a very efficient gunner regiment. On one such exercise we spent a night in the open in the park at Luton. It rained all that night and I had a streaming cold, which was probably influenza and this had gone to my chest. Early the following morning I was ordered to take a car and drive up to London for an RAF medical examination. By reason of my chest condition the junior medical officer refused to pass me but the senior medical officer thereupon did pass me. I mention this because it shows that the RAF were then desperate to get pilots without any delay.

After this I was sent on a battery commander's course at Ilkley in Yorkshire. By this time it was believed that the Germans would not invade until after the winter because the Battle of Britain had prevented their planned autumn invasion. I was given enough petrol coupons to

11

take my Rover fourteen there and back: travelling by train was unmitigated hell in those days. I had discovered this a month or so before when I had gone by train on a week's leave to my home in Angus. Though officers were granted vouchers for first class tickets there was no class or rank on trains at that time. Every train was packed with people who stood, compressed together like sardines in a tin, in every compartment and corridor. My journey home had taken about fourteen hours each way and trains were liable to stop for indefinite periods because 'the engine had run out of steam'. The trains had to be completely blacked out after dark and as the stations were all in complete darkness and had no boards which identified them, it was extremely difficult to discover when one had arrived at one's destination.

Arriving by car in Ilkley was like arriving in another world. Whereas life in the South of England had been all work and no play, there was abundant play in Ilkley. During that course there were two dances and many dinner parties and on two occasions I took new girl friends to dine and dance at a luxury hotel which I think was in Harrogate. I was told that shortly before the outbreak of war a certain Luftwaffe pilot had been thrown out of the hotel because of his behaviour and he had sworn that he would take his revenge. Much later I heard that the hotel had been demolished by a German bomb and that this had been attributed to that pilot.

Perhaps I should add that there was (unfortunately) no permissive society in those days and seducing married women whose husbands were serving overseas was regarded as despicable.

The countryside in the neighbourhood of Ilkley was quite lovely and very suitable for TEWTs (ie Tactical Exercises Without Troops) and the instructors were all most helpful. The course was run by Jerry Shiel who was later CRA of the 51st Highland Division during the France/Germany Campaign when he was one of my best customers for photographs of the enemy front line and weapon pits and he had copies of these distributed down to platoon commanders. He was, alas, killed before the Campaign ended.

When that course was completed I was ordered to go straight to an EFTS (Elementary Flying Training School) at Woodley near Reading.

CHAPTER IV

The Early Days of the Air OP

Charles Bazeley had no opportunity during the brief fighting which preceded the fall of France to demonstrate the potential value of an Air Observation Post. And after Dunkirk the politicians and the War Office were far too busy to think about anything so long term as an Air OP. But after the Battle of Britain and the later destruction by bombing of invasion barges which had been assembled by the Germans on the other side of the Channel, it appeared that the expected invasion was no longer quite so imminent. Charles kept on persevering and won some support from some gunners at the War Office with the result that a trickle of gunner officers started to be sent for flying training.

But the Air Ministry was becoming increasingly aware of the potential threat to the Royal Air Force. The Royal Flying Corps of the First World War had been a part of the Army. Under Lord Trenchard the RFC had had to fight hard to win their independence from the Army and many of the officers who had fought and won that political battle were in the Air Ministry or Air Marshals elsewhere, during the Second World War. They had no intention of allowing all that they had achieved to be thrown away. So they insisted that any officer who flew aircraft must be under the command of the RAF, and that only RAF personnel could maintain and service aircraft.

For some considerable time it had been possible for an Army officer to apply to be seconded to the RAF for a period of years. Charles Bazeley had done this before the War began. Secondment meant that the officer changed from brown uniform into blue and became in every way under the command of the RAF. He wore RAF wings and was paid by the RAF. So the Air Ministry argued that Air OP officers should likewise be seconded. But the Army argued that they wanted fully trained gunner officers who would fly light aircraft and operate from fields just behind the Army front line and would wear brown and be under the command of the Army. These arguments caused long delays and during the early part of 1941 there were successive periods of doubt as to whether the Air OP would ever get off the ground.

Eventually a nebulous agreement was reached whereby we were to be 'brown jobs' in RAF squadrons and under RAF command and discipline but we were to be under the 'operational command' of the Army. In this way the Army would believe that we were Army officers who would do whatever the Army ordered us to do but the RAF would know that we were in fact part of them. We were to be 'lent' by the Army to the RAF instead of being 'seconded' to them.

There were certain disadvantages to us Air OP pilots in this arrangement. As we were only being 'lent' to the RAF we were not entitled to RAF wings and it was years before our Air OP wings had been designed and approved. Neither the Royal Navy nor the RAF could understand Army officers without wings who landed at their air stations from time to time to refuel or stay overnight. They thought we must be pupils whose flights had to be 'authorised'. I will describe later an argument which I had in November 1941 with the Naval 'Commander Flying' at Worthy Down.

Then there was the matter of flying pay. We were paid by the Army Pay Office and they knew of no such thing as flying pay. After a year or two it was decided that we were to be paid two shillings a day 'extra danger pay' in lieu of flying pay. No tax was deducted from this as it was believed to be a tax-free allowance. But at the end of the War the tax people changed their wretched minds and insisted that, as it had been described as 'pay' it should have been taxed. As a result almost all of my demobilisation gratuity was withheld due to the alleged tax which had, through their negligence, not been deducted at time of payment.

On the other hand I think the advantages of being 'lent' to the RAF vastly exceeded the disadvantages. The RAF understood pilots far better than did the Army. The RAF were fully aware that courage is an expendable commodity, like an electric battery which has to be recharged at regular intervals. A pilot, who 'dices with death' all day long and sometimes at night also, was given a week's leave every six weeks in order to keep his courage going (whereas in the Army it was a week's leave every twelve weeks), and RAF pilots were fed like fighting cocks with 'aircrew rations'.

There was a story that a certain 'chairborne' group captain shortly after the Battle of Britain, gave a young fighter pilot a rocket for not having the top button of his tunic done up and for not having saluted him, a senior officer. The fighter pilot replied, 'Shut up, you bloody penguin'. The question thereupon arose as to whether the fighter pilot should be disciplined for his behaviour but the RAF higher command understood and it was the group captain who got a rocket.

Here I am going to digress and tell a Naval story which illustrates the point which I have made above. A Fleet Air Arm pilot took off from his carrier somewhere in the Mediterranean to carry out some operational sortie. There was wireless silence which meant that he could not under any circumstance communicate with his carrier. He got lost and so he did the prescribed 'square searches' in order to find the carrier but he failed to do so. When he had only a few minutes' fuel left he saw the carrier in the distance. While he was flying towards it he was expecting his fuel to be exhausted at any moment. In fact he landed just before his fuel would have run out. The captain of the carrier, who had never flown an aircraft, had been waiting anxiously for him and gave him an imperial rocket as soon as he got out of the aircraft. The pilot, who was emotionally exhausted, replied by telling the captain precisely what he thought of him. The Senior Service did not tolerate such impudence and the pilot was court-martialled.

The president of the court martial was a friend of my family and it was he who told me this story. The pilot was acquitted and the captain was told that in future he must allow pilots to calm down and rest before he reprimanded them.

It must not be thought from what I have said above that the RAF lacked discipline. Any commanding officer could send an undisciplined pilot on the 'Brighton Course'. This was a fortnight's course in discipline at Brighton which was dreaded by all RAF pilots because, though it was a course and not officially a punishment, life there was rather like being at an Army 'glasshouse'. I myself never needed to send any officer on that course because I never detected any offence which justified such drastic action. But the fact that the course was available certainly acted as a deterrent. I know of one or two Air OP officers who were sent there. The great advantage of this course was that as it was not officially a punishment it was no blemish on an officer's record.

In 1943, I lunched with the Judge Advocate General, Col Edward Betts, to the American

14

Forces in Europe who was a friend of my family. I told him of the Brighton Course and he thought it an excellent idea and said that he would recommend that a similar course be instituted for the American Forces. This reminds me of a day in October 1944 when I flew the American Liaison Officer at Tac HQ Second Army to see General Hodges, the Commander of the 1st American Army, at Verviers. An American fighter pilot beat up (they called it 'buzzing') General Hodges' HQ in an outrageous manner. Finally the General could stand no more of it and he gave the order 'Rub him out'. Thereupon they shot down their own undisciplined pilot.

Having mentioned Lord Trenchard, I will now tell a story about him. As he was the Father of the RAF and a fine old boy, they dug him out of retirement and sent him on a tour of RAF stations in order to boost morale. He was habitually most charming. Unfortunately, as happens to all of us as we grow old, his memory of people's names and identities had gone. So he made a habit of going up to officers at parties in RAF Messes, holding out his hand for a handshake and at the same time saying, 'I know you. We met at ... where was it?' The other chap would then identify himself and might feel pleased that the great Marshal of the RAF had remembered him. One day at the end of such a party the great man went up to a young officer whose face seemed familiar, shook him by the hand and went through the usual routine. The young man replied, 'Yes Sir, I am your ADC.'

At the beginning of November 1940, I drove south from Ilkley in my Rover fourteen, having fortunately obtained some more petrol coupons there, and began a course at No.8 Elementary and Reserve Flying Training School at Woodley near Reading. There were thirty-five of us on that course of whom only four or five were gunner officers destined for the Air OP. Almost all the remainder were Army officers who were being seconded to the RAF, which we gunner officers were not permitted to be. I learned later that all, or almost all, of the seconded officers did not survive the War. I am writing this part of my memoirs forty years later and it now seems strange to me that we should all have been so keen to apply when we knew that our prospects of survival would be remote. People felt that way in 1940. I remember having been exasperated when an American girl whom I had met in Ilkley said to me that Britain could not possibly win the War. Of course we British always won our wars in the end.

We were to be trained on Magisters or 'Maggies'. This was a low-wing monoplane which was a delight to fly. It was not a particularly safe aircraft for beginners as, if misused, it would go into a spin far more easily than an Avro would have done. One could not have done a 'falling leaf' in a Maggie. When one went into a spin in a Maggie, one had to put the stick right forward before applying opposite rudder. If one failed to remember this necessity, the aircraft would not come out of the spin. In the early days of our course, one of us and his instructor were killed when their aircraft spun and crashed beside the airfield. When one goes into a spin at a height below 2,000 feet it is obviously very difficult to make oneself put the stick right forward before applying opposite rudder.

But the Magister was a suitable aircraft for preparing pilots to fly the Master at an SFTS (Senior Flying Training School). The Master was a fighter trainer and a notorious killer of inexperienced pilots. In February 1942, Evelyn Prendergast and I went to Cambridge for a two-month Flying Instructors' Course where we flew only in the Magister or the DH82. But we wanted to have a go at flying a Master. So on the 24th of September 1942, we flew together to Cambridge on a 'Map Reading Exercise' and persuaded the Chief Instructor, S/Ldr Beardon, to 'convert' us to the Master. The instructors at Cambridge were particularly friendly and helpful, and Beardon went up with us in turn for forty-five minutes each.

By then we were of course very experienced pilots. It was enormous fun flying at the speed of a fighter, doing flick-rolls as well as the usual aerobatics. But the problem was coming in to land, and Beardon was perhaps a brave man in leaving the landings entirely to us, as Cambridge was a small grass airfield with no runway and the airfield was covered with Magisters and Tiger Moths taxiing after landing. Compared with the aircraft which we were accustomed to fly, the Master sank like a lift during the approach and landed at great speed while I hoped that no aircraft failed to notice my approach and taxied across my path.

I have written at some length about the Master as I am now going to refer to what I think was one of the Air Ministry's greatest blunders during the War. The fault may of course have been that of the Flying Training Command but we then attributed all blunders to the Air Ministry which we called 'the Lap of the Gods'. At that time fully trained pilots were needed desperately. We heard of one Senior Flying Training School at Hullavington and one at Montrose – there may have been others elsewhere. Every pupil at an SFTS had to do a certain amount of night flying when he was certainly not ready for this. The order may have been reasonable during the summer months but in the winter, when low cloud or mist might arrive unexpectedly at any time, the casualties from night flying in Masters were quite appalling. When I was at Reading in November and December 1940 there were stories circulating of courses at Hullavington and Montrose during which more than half the pupil pilots were killed. Montrose was probably the worst because there the 'Ha' (ie mist) habitually comes in from the sea at night and frequently during the day also.

A feature of our course at Reading was the outrageous behaviour of a few of its members in Sonning and elsewhere during the evenings. There was one wild Irishman who was a particular offender and some of his exploits were rather amusing such as when he caused chaos at a wedding reception in Sonning. It was so unlike an Army course where everyone behaved correctly. The CO, W/Cdr Moir, lectured us all on this subject on several occasions but to no avail. These few offenders had accepted that their lives would be short and were determined to enjoy them to the full.

As I write I am remembering David Hawkins, son of Anthony Hope Hawkins the novelist who wrote *The Prisoner of Zenda*. David was a magnificent young man in every way. He radiated friendship towards all men, and his eyes were always full of merriment. He survived the SFTS and was then sent to an operational squadron of light bombers which bombed enemy shipping. This was a suicide task as, in order to be effective, they had to approach enemy ships at little more than mast height in order to drop bombs on them. I heard not long afterwards that David had been killed.

While at Woodley we all stayed in the Falcon which was next to the airfield. It was most luxurious and I think it had been the clubhouse of a flying club before the War. We were fed like fighting cocks and this was presumably because we had become entitled to aircrew rations. In the evenings, geese used to come from the Thames and fly past the Falcon and as Harry Scott and I had shotguns with us we brought some of them down.

We had to learn to read Aldis lamp signals in morse code which was of no practical value to Air OP officers. We all had flying tests by the CO and on one of these tests the CO mentioned casually to one of us who was being tested, 'If you look over the port side you will see enemy bombs now falling on the aerodrome'. On almost every night we listened to vast numbers of enemy bombers going over us on their way to attack somewhere in the Midlands.

At the end of the course there was a written examination which was important because if we failed it we would be sent back to our regiments which we considered to be a fate worse than death. Of course those who set the examination wanted us all to pass, as pilots were needed so desperately. The various subjects were 'met' which included the types of cloud which we should avoid flying into, engines, airframes and navigation. So far as I remember, the navigation exam lasted two hours and involved a great deal of plotting courses so as to allow for direction and strength of wind, magnetic variation, etc. Macrae, a gunner officer who had been an actuary before the War, took out his slide rule, worked out all the answers with almost the speed of a computer, wrote them down without bothering to show how he had arrived at them and then walked out of the room after a mere ten minutes. The invigilator assumed that he was walking out because the questions were too difficult for him and tried to persuade him to stay and go on trying as otherwise he would have to be failed. The examiner obviously did not like answers which, although entirely correct, did not show the prescribed manner in which they should have been arrived at, as Macrae's name was near the bottom of the list of those who had passed. I do not think that anyone failed.

By reason of the fact that I had taken those exams during my two years with the Cambridge University Air Squadron, I passed out top. But there had been a few differences in my previous exam in 1932. Then there were still a few airships and we had to learn how to avoid colliding with them as they had absolute priority. I vaguely remember that if an airship was seen hanging out two small black balls it meant that one had to keep a certain distance from it, and two large black balls meant a greater distance. In my previous exam when with the CUAS there was a question, 'What does it mean when an airship hangs out two large black balls?' One member of the CUAS did not know the answer and so wrote down, 'It means that the Aga Khan is on board.'

At the end of that course I went north for Christmas on a week's leave before returning to London where I took my Rover fourteen down to Fort Burgoyne, near Dover. I heard that the formation of an Air OP had been postponed indefinitely and I was ordered to return to my Regiment. It was not until the 1st of June 1941 that I was summoned to Larkhill for further Air OP training. This delay led both Harry Scott and Macrae to give up altogether their intention of joining the Air OP. The next time I saw Harry he was standing beside a tank during the liberation of Brussels.

CHAPTER V

Fort Burgoyne

When I set off by car to go from London to Dover the road seemed completely empty. The South-East of England had become an exclusion zone and no one could get into it unless he was on duty there. I came to a barrier where I had to show my identity card and explain where I was going. My car had very little petrol left and it had become badly in need of major repairs. I had to use all my newly acquired mechanical knowledge to keep it going at all. But I somehow got it to my destination. From this time on one was not accepted just because one was in uniform: one had to be prepared to produce one's identity card wherever one went. The loss of one's identity card necessitated a Court of Inquiry. The loss of one's revolver was a terrible offence.

Fort Burgoyne was built during the Napoleonic wars to resist a possible invasion by the French. It was surrounded by a dry moat, and in parts of the moat minefields had been laid. The location of each individual mine was marked by a strip of wire which appeared above the ground. This was presumably to facilitate their eventual clearance but it did seem to limit the effectiveness of these minefields except to strangers who entered the moat in the dark.

There was also a great deal of dannert wire in the moat. Dannert wire was barbed wire wound round and round and with a diameter of about four feet. It was really no obstacle at all as, with a little practice, one could trample it down and then walk over it. But one could not run through it. The brick walls of the fort rose to a height of about thirty feet and on the side which faced France a wall of earth had been erected behind and up to perhaps fifteen feet above the brick wall. Presumably this wall of earth had been put there to strengthen the brick wall against cannonballs. On the top of this wall of earth was a place where an officer had to be not only by day but all through every night to watch for and give immediate warning of the first sign of the expected invasion.

For this purpose every officer of whatever rank had to take turns to do four-hour watches. This was not a very pleasant job in winter in the early hours of the morning when it was snowing or there was a thick fog but the fact that visibility was down to only a few yards was no reason to cease to maintain this watch. Fortunately for me I had retained my flying clothing and my sheep's wool lined leather flying boots. After coming off watch we used to drink a tumblerful of rum and milk – fifty per cent of each. I never liked rum but this did warm one up before going to bed.

The entrance to the fort was by a narrow wooden bridge where a sentry stood and demanded to see the identity card of everyone not personally known to him who wished to enter the fort. The rooms in the fort all had bare stone walls and floors and practically no furniture. Damp was everywhere. In the Mess was a blackboard on which was written in chalk the names in rotation of the next twelve officers due to go on leave. This was somewhat depressing when one's name was near the bottom of the list. We all knew that once the invasion began none of us would be likely ever to go on leave again. The meals were very austere compared with the meals that I had become accustomed to when with the RAF. But the cook did keep a flock of geese which had provided a Christmas dinner for everyone in the battery, though I myself had not arrived there until shortly after Christmas. The Dorchester battery were quartered elsewhere and I scarcely ever saw them again. I don't even know where they were.

Every man in the battery, both officers and men, worked hard preparing places for each of the twelve 25-pounder guns of the battery in the earth mound above the wall which faced the sea. The soil removed had to be shovelled into sandbags and carried away.

Our orders were that every gun of the battery had to be kept loaded and layed on our defensive fire tasks. The defensive fire task of my 'E' Troop was the farmhouse near St Margaret's Bay. Our orders were that as soon as a golden rain rocket appeared in the sky to signal that the invasion had begun, every gun, without any further order, was immediately to fire a considerable number of rounds on its defensive fire task. I understand that every artillery gun in South-East England had the same orders, except of course that their targets were different. In this manner a hail of shells was intended to cover all the likely invasion beaches and all the buildings which the German troops would be likely to occupy shortly after they had landed. We were not sure as to what a golden rain rocket looked like and we referred to it as 'the flaming raspberry'.

I thought then and I still think now, that these orders were completely absurd. It seemed quite pointless to demolish buildings before the Germans got there. Most of the guns of South-East England had targets on the beaches but since the beaches were protected by mines, it was surely pointless to assist the enemy by exploding all the mines before they set foot on the shore. Of course much would depend on the timing of the golden rain rocket. Surely the orders should have been that the fire of our guns should be controlled by orders given by our own officers in their observation posts.

I took my troop on a route march to have a look at the farmhouse which we were to demolish as soon as the Germans landed. It was still being occupied and there was a most attractive farmer's daughter or 'land girl' whom we all admired. That girl never knew it, but she probably saved Britain losing the War. Late one night when I was on watch on the battlements the golden rain rocket appeared: our orders were that it was to be the signal for us to start firing. If we had fired, it is probable that every other gun in South-East England would also have started firing. The battle would have begun before there was any enemy to fight. But the men were thinking about the occupants of that farmhouse. We were all a bit trigger-happy but the men were not going to fire until they had received a direct order from me. I telephoned Brigade Headquarters in Dover Castle and they confirmed that we should not fire until we received further orders. Later they rang back to say that a barrage balloon had broken loose from its moorings and its wire cable had become entangled in some high tension wires thereby giving rise to a shower of sparks. We could not be blamed for having confused this with the golden rain rocket which we had never seen. I should perhaps add that, despite our orders, I would never have dared to be the first to open fire even if a genuine golden rain rocket had appeared.

At the top of a long hill which led from Fort Burgoyne to Dover a very large barrel filled with a highly inflammable mixture of oil had been placed beside the road. The idea was that a tap at the bottom of the barrel should be opened and the oil set on fire as soon as enemy troops appeared at the bottom of this hill. As a result the enemy vehicles coming up the hill would be set on fire also. What in fact happened was that this barrel leaked and the road down the hill became covered with oil which fortunately did not ignite. I, in my folly, imagined that this oil mixture was petrol and as I already had a bad oil stain on my battle-dress, I tried to remove this oil stain with this 'petrol'. As a result my battledress got in a hell of a mess. A replacement not being then obtainable from stores, I wrote to my tailors, Hunts-man of Savile Row and asked them to make me a battledress according to my measurements which they of course had and to send it to me as quickly as possible. They sent it to me with amazing speed and I, when in battledress, was thereafter probably the best dressed officer in the Army. Fortunately, we then always wore denims for any dirty jobs or manual labour.

When General Montgomery, as he then was, became Commander of all troops in the South-East of England, our divisional commander was retired. I met him shortly afterwards and he was then a sergeant in the Home Guard, which was at that time known as the LDVs which I believe meant Land Defence Volunteers. He was armed only with his shotgun and the men under him were armed with an assortment of weapons such as pitchforks and ancient pikes. I admired his spirit.

Montgomery summoned all the officers under him, except of course the orderly officers, to the Odeon Cinema in Folkestone in order to hear him give a lecture. I wonder what would have happened in the War if a German bomb had landed on that cinema while we were all in it. Montgomery's aim from then until the end of the War appeared to be to convince all those under him that he was an invincible general. Perhaps he was justified in this. He addressed us from the stage and began by saying that he would give his audience two minutes in which to cough and that after that no one would cough while he was speaking. He also said that no one was to smoke.

We junior officers were at the back of the house but the senior officers in the front rows were probably more concerned with the necessity of not coughing than with listening to what the General was saying. The General did say that he had recently visited a regiment and there had asked a junior officer what 'pill-boxes' he had. The junior officer replied, 'I have one over there which was sited by my Company Commander, one over there which was sited by the Colonel and a third one over there which was sited by the Brigadier.' Mont-gomery then asked, 'Which of them will you use when the fighting starts?' The junior officer replied, 'None of them: they are all in the wrong places.' Having told this story, Mont-gomery assured us that no senior officers under his command would ever make any such decisions which should properly be left to junior officers who were to fight the battle. Apart from this the General did not say anything that seemed to us to be of any importance and we all felt that our journey to Folkestone had been a waste of petrol.

The word 'Cromwell' was a magic top secret word at that time. It was so top secret that we were not told whether it meant that the Germans had already landed or that it meant merely that an invasion was believed to be imminent. It was a code word that was never to be uttered for fear of it coming to the ears of the enemy. I was later told a delightful story by someone who had been at this time on the staff of a Major-General who was commanding a district somewhere in the North of England.

During the War the Mecca of all officers on leave was London. This is perhaps not sur-prising as the grand hotels, such as the Dorchester, Grosvenor, Savoy, Mayfair, etc, charged officers only nominal prices for their bedrooms and there was a maximum lawful charge of five shillings for any meal – though champagne cost £5 a bottle and teetotallers were not very popular. The fact that London was being consistently bombed was no deterrent at all: in fact the excitement of being bombed added to the other attractions. London was the place where one met one's girl friends, even though they were not living there either. I remember one evening when I was in a bath in the Dorchester when the guns in Hyde Park were being heavily bombed during a particularly severe raid. That great hotel shook to its foundations and I decided that I did not want to be found naked in the rubble. So I got out of my bath and put some clothes on.

This Major-General was no exception. He came down to London from the North in his staff car to spend one or two nights at the Savoy with a young and glamorous girl friend. One night when they were in bed together the telephone in his bedroom rang and he found that the staff officer (who told me this story) was at the other end of the line. The staff officer had to invent a code as the word 'Cromwell' must never be uttered. So he said, 'I am terribly sorry, Sir, to have to bother you at this time of night, but a gentleman who was associated with Charles I has just called. I will get in touch with your driver and tell him to have your car outside the Savoy as soon as possible.'

Now the Major-General had no leave or authority to go outside his District during that critical time. He leaped out of bed, dressed hurriedly and set off in his staff car to drive all through the night back to his District. Though this Cromwell alert afterwards proved to be a false alarm, the entire Home Guard had also been alerted and they had set up road blocks on all the main roads.

The Major-General was in far too much of a hurry to bother about the Home Guard, nor was he anxious to explain to anyone the reason for his journey. So when they reached a road block he ordered his driver to drive through without stopping. A Home Guard sentry, after his shout of 'Halt, or I fire!' had been totally ignored, shot the Major-General in the bottom from which wound he bled profusely. The driver of course stopped and the sentry then put his head through the car window and undismayed by his target's august uniform, said, 'It is just as well that you did stop as next time I would have shot to kill.'

The sequel to this story is that this District Commander was 'broken'. I have no information as to whether or not he then joined the Home Guard.

As I had learned ju-jitsu while I was at Cambridge, I became an instructor in unarmed combat. I had in my troop a driver named Wynne who was 6 feet 4 inches in height, of magnificent physique, as strong as Hercules and had been an 'all-in wrestler' before the War. He was also extremely gentle and friendly by nature. I thought the world of him. He and I together gave demonstrations of unarmed combat and taught this to a number of gunners who were interested. The most difficult task was to make people keep absolutely silent when moving in the dark in a practice raid. While we were at St Albans I had taken my troop to Bricket Wood and had ordered them to move in a line through a thick wood in the pitch dark. I found that I could not stop them calling incessantly to each other: perhaps each of them was afraid of getting lost. My commandos had to learn to keep silent and to move silently so as to take an enemy by surprise.

One night I was ordered to arrange at short notice a demonstration of commando warfare which the Colonel would watch. The night was very dark and I had to think up something quickly. So I announced that there was a German spy, represented by myself, hiding somewhere in the moat and that Wynne and three other commandos were to search the moat, in complete silence, without any torches and catch this spy and bring him up the wall into the fort for interrogation. The only way from the moat up to where we were standing in the fort was by rope up the 30-foot wall. I emphasized that there was a great deal of dannert wire in the moat but that this should present no difficulty even in the dark and that I didn't want anyone to blunder into a minefield. I told my commandos to give me ten minutes' start and then I fixed a long rope to the top of the wall, climbed down into the moat and disappeared into the darkness.

That game was rather more exciting than I had anticipated. I hid somewhere, and then began to worry lest someone trod on a mine in which event I would be responsible for his death. The commandos searched very slowly and in complete silence. Eventually I heard a very faint sound of movement close to me and so I got up and ran. Suddenly I was tackled and brought down, my hands and feet were tied and then I was thrown across Wynne's massive shoulders and carried back to where the rope was hanging. On the way Wynne had to step across some dannert wire while he was carrying me – which shows how ineffective dannert wire really was. They tied me to the end of the rope and hauled me up into the fort – unhurt.

At about that time General Allfrey became our divisional commander. He had been a gunner and he was everything that a general should be. Word got round that he was inspecting each regiment in turn and that his inspections were extremely thorough. Static warfare was bad for training and for morale. For example, one officer was living in an observation post at St Margaret's Bay, another at the top of the tower of the Duke of York's School and a third in a pill-box near the top of a hill from which there was a magnificent view. Telephone lines were layed to each of these OPs. During his first day in an OP the officer would draw a large and artistic panorama of everything that he could see and would set out the range from the guns, etc to each landmark or other possible target. Thereafter he had very little to do but prepare his own meals, read library books, or gaze into the distance and contemplate infinity.

His successor in the OP would be tempted to take over the existing panoramic sketch and not bother to learn the countryside within his field of view. Then there would be serious trouble when General Allfrey asked the OP officer to name every church, every village, every copse and every other landmark within sight. Col Woodward and Roscoe Turner kept us all up to the mark and we had nothing to fear from any inspection. General Allfrey stopped the nonsense of the flaming raspberry and the defensive fire tasks. We had great confidence in him. General Montgomery had a genius for picking the right men to serve under him.

Montgomery himself paid some surprise, and sometimes embarrassing, visits to the regiments under his command. We heard that he had arrived without warning at 0800 hrs at one unit. He found a squad of men on parade waiting for the appearance of their officer who was still in his bedroom shaving. When this officer did appear, the indignant General said to him, 'I see you are a captain. Tomorrow you will be only a lieutenant.'

Montgomery was very quick to break any officer, of whatever rank, who displeased him. On one occasion he visited a regiment whose Colonel had been a cavalry officer: the General was not fond of cavalry officers. They spoke together for only ten minutes and the General asked the Colonel what he had done between the Wars. The Colonel started talking about hunting, fishing and shooting, which was the worst possible thing he could have said. The correct answer would have been that he had studied military history and had visited the places where famous battles had been fought. Such an answer would have led to a most enjoyable conversation. So Montgomery put in an adverse report on this Colonel so that he might be broken. The Colonel was of course entitled to see this report and he wrote on it, 'General Montgomery visited my regiment for only ten minutes all of which he spent in the Mess.' To this the General added the words, 'Ten minutes was enough.' I heard this story from an uncle of mine who dealt with this matter at the War Office. Of course the Colonel was broken: no one thwarted Montgomery.

We learned that the Regiment was to take part in an exercise to be held by the Division on a lonely part of the shore of Kent. We were to fire a lifting barrage while the infantry, accompanied by General Allfrey himself, were to advance close behind this barrage. Heavy machine-guns were meanwhile to fire from each flank just over the heads of the infantry or in front of them. We thought the General a brave man as a single error by a gun layer would have resulted in a shell falling short and thereby causing heavy casualties. I was a troop commander and during the firing of a lifting barrage a troop commander has precisely nothing to do except worry. He has to leave the supervision of the gunners to his GPO (Gun Position Officer). I was extremely worried but everything went like clockwork that day.

The Germans used to shell Dover from time to time from the French coast. The shells travelled faster than the speed of sound and this meant that we saw and heard the bursts before we heard the shells coming. This seemed most strange. Whenever shelling started we used to hurry down to the town from the fort in order to check and if necessary repair any severed telephone cables. Our communications had at all times to be in working order. On such occasions Dover seemed a ghost town, the streets being entirely deserted except by us.

In due course I became battery captain. One day Roscoe took me with him to watch a demonstration, which was being given for Churchill and the Commander-in-Chief Home Forces then General Sir Alan Brooke, of Britain's largest gun firing at Calais in retaliation for the many shells which had landed in Dover. This gigantic gun normally lived on a railway line in a tunnel near Dover, but it was brought out for this demonstration. It was very inaccurate in its MPI (Mean Point of Impact) and it almost certainly could not be expected to hit an enemy gun emplacement or an enemy battleship passing through the Straits of Dover. It could be expected to hit the city of Calais: though where the shells landed in Calais was anyone's guess. It was being fired to boost the morale of the citizens of Dover by showing them that the enemy were being given a taste of their own medicine. This seemed quite absurd to me as, whereas the Germans had been firing at us – their enemies, we were firing at a city of our friends and allies. What stupid things are done in war in the name of boosting morale. I wonder if our gun ever killed a single German. The actual effect of firing our gun was to encourage the German gun or guns to fire considerably more shells at us.

Frequently we watched fights overhead between Spitfires and enemy fighters. To our disgust the enemy generally appeared to win these fights but then the enemy aircraft outnumbered our own. When our pilots descended by parachute we watched to make sure that they landed on land and not in the sea. How I longed to get back to flying. But it was not until the 1st of June 1941 that I was summoned to Larkhill to complete my training as an Air OP pilot.

I simply loved flying. There are few things, if any, in life so satisfying as flying a light aircraft, whether it be skimming along the tops of clouds shining in the sunlight, flying just over the tops of the trees, or flying high and seeing the countryside far below. One learns to understand the clouds, the winds, the storms, the mists and the sunsets. One sees the earth below in a god-like perspective. Men seem like ants pursuing their trivial tasks. All petty things are seen to be what they really are. Ambition and enmity become irrelevant. Death itself seems merely an event which will enable one to fly without the necessity of an aircraft.

I wrote these Memoirs during the War. Now, forty years on, I have been tempted to delete the last paragraph because it must seem rather silly today. But I have decided to leave it in as it shows how we, or at any rate I, felt during the War. Nowadays most people seem to believe that death is the end and that this means that life must be preserved as long as possible, even after it has ceased to be worth living. People say that those who are born mentally handicapped, paralysed and in constant pain have a right to live for as long as the medical profession can possibly preserve their lives. We did not think this way during the last War, or how could we have daily 'diced with death' for so many years. These absurd modern beliefs have never been held before throughout recorded history. People now seem to have no time or wish to think deeply.

I, and many others like me, have always been absolutely convinced that death is not the end but the goal of life. Life is like a term at school and when we die we go home for the holidays. It is not for us to speculate as to what happens to us after death. It is enough for us to know that we are immortal souls. When I remember my friends who gave their lives so willingly in the War, I like to think that when they passed the gates, or tunnel, of death 'all the trumpets sounded for them on the other side'.

CHAPTER VI
'D' Flight RAF

In the spring of 1941 we were beginning to become a bit tired of waiting for an invasion which never came. So I obtained leave to go to Larkhill to try to find out there whether there was going to be an Air OP or not. Mike Lees, who had been my troop GPO, intended to volunteer for the Special Air Service and I might have done likewise if the Air OP had been abandoned. Incidentally Mike was later seriously wounded in an SAS raid on General Kesselring's HQ in Italy when, I understand, they were attempting to take Kesselring prisoner.

I went by train from Dover to Amesbury and walked to Larkhill from the station. My Rover was completely out of action: at any rate I thought so, but I later discovered that its cylinders had been rebored and it had been made almost as new in complete secrecy by my troop motor mechanic in his spare time – he was the one who had been Lord Digby's chauffeur, Bdr Chapman.

I found Charles Bazeley in a wooden hut by the small grass airfield. He was wearing the uniform of an RAF squadron leader. He explained the then situation to me and said that it would not be long before I was summoned to Larkhill for an Air OP course. He drove me back to Amesbury Railway Station.

I understand that Jim Neathercoat and Ralph Cobley had been trained by Eric Joyce and Roddy Davenport during that period of uncertainty. I do not think either of them ever went to an EFTS. Certainly these two were the first of the Air OP pilots. As they were not members of any recognized Army establishment, there was no possibility of their ever being promoted captains until a much later date when 651 Air OP Squadron was eventually formed in August 1941. This was a pity.

It is said that Charles allowed Ralph to select the names for the First AOP Course and that Ralph took care to pick only subalterns as he was a very ambitious man and did not want to risk being superseded by a captain. The First Course were all subalterns – Tetley Tetley-Jones, John Ingram, Norman Lane, Terry Willet and Monkey Morgan. We saw very little of them during our Second Course as they were constantly touring the country giving demonstrations of Air OP shoots. They all later became Air OP squadron commanders except A. C. Morgan (always known as 'Monkey') who crashed during Exercise Bumper and was never fit to fly again.

It is said that Charles himself picked the names for the Second Course. This consisted of three captains, Bill Ballard, Hugh Barber and myself and three subalterns, Evelyn Prendergast, Geoffrey Pollitt and Bob Harker. Ralph gave us captains a rough time. Hugh once said that he was 'not going to be spoken to like that by a subaltern', and this was a bad mistake. So Hugh failed the course and was sent back to his regiment. I suspect that I also might have been failed had I not been under Jim Neathercoat, instead of under Ralph, during the final exercise.

25

I think the Air OP owed far more to Jim Neathercoat than to any other man, except of course Charles Bazeley. Jim was calm, casual and confident at all times, however great the emergency. He was friendly and helpful to those under him and won their affection. And he never asked anyone under him to do anything that he was not willing to do himself. During the early months of the Air OP we were all constantly learning to do something which had never been done before – 'short landings' into small fields. The RAF had taught pilots to do forced or emergency landings in authorised fields, but they had never even heard of short landings because none of their aircraft were capable of them, apart from the Tiger Moth which was used only as a training aircraft for beginners. And the RAF had never needed to do short landings.

During those early months when we were flying pre-war civilian aircraft of considerable age and very doubtful performance, there was one problem which was constantly arising. A flight of our aircraft would land successfully by short landings in a small field, perhaps uphill here or downhill there, with a wood on one side, scattered trees on two sides, and telephone wires or HT (high tension) cables on the fourth side and perhaps with a dew pond or some boggy ground in it. The wind strength and direction had been right when they had landed, each pilot having done the prescribed 'dummy run' over his chosen landing path between two trees before he landed in order to make quite sure that the surface was right. Then, perhaps the same day or the following day, they all wondered whether or not it would be possible for them to take off again.

This could be an alarming problem for inexperienced pilots. The wind might have changed in strength or direction during the night. Rain might have made the ground water-logged. We would pace the length of a chosen take-off path, face into the wind so as to sense its strength and direction, and consider carefully the softness of the ground. Then would be the time for someone to 'have a go' at taking off. Jim, as flight commander and the most experienced AOP pilot, always took off first. This became the established rule in the Air OP.

As I write this, I am remembering Jim on our final two-day exercise during that course. We had only one aircraft, a Piper Cub, between three of us. I see from my log book that the date was the 7th/8th of July 1941. That evening Jim showed us how to picket the aircraft down on top of a hill on Salisbury Plain. Then he told us that cows eat aircraft – actually they lick the dope and this removes all the fabric. Horses sometimes destroy aircraft by rubbing their bottoms against them. So we found some ancient barbed wire and disused fencing posts and constructed a makeshift fence around the aircraft to protect it during the night.

I never did such a thing again. I found it far easier to go and call on the farmer, be as charming to him as I possibly could and persuade him to move the cows from that field. Or better still, I would send Montagu to see the farmer. Montagu could charm anyone, even Yorkshire farmers.

Our instruction was primarily directed to teaching us the art of doing Air OP shoots and short landings. We had of course already had a great deal of experience in doing shoots from the ground and I had even done a shoot with naval guns at a floating target out at sea. On the ground one could use field-glasses and had nothing much more to do than spot the fall of the shells and apply the prescribed rules of ranging, concentration, etc. But when flying an aircraft it was much more difficult. We had to fly the aircraft just above the ground so as to keep out of sight of the imaginary enemy and it was then necessary in order to switch from send to receive, or vice versa, to turn right round to the wireless set behind us and move a lever on the set up or down. During this operation we had to take our eyes off where we were going. We had to climb up steeply to observe the fall of each ranging round and of the fire for effect.

Immediately after each fall of shot we had to dive down again to just above ground level and from there give the next order.

It was this diving down that was likely to cause crashes. It was only natural that pilots would try to fly in a spectacular manner when doing demonstration shoots. When one pulls out of a dive the aircraft sinks faster and further than one would expect. And the steeper the dive the further the sink. I realized this when I was CGI at Old Sarum and was doing a demonstration shoot for some foreign military mission. On one dive in my Taylorcraft I sank so far and fast that I only just missed hitting the ground. Peter Kroyer learned this lesson the hard way. When he was in my Squadron and doing a demonstration shoot at Hawk Down, he dived into the ground. He told me that his life was saved by the engine and the rest of the aircraft ending up some distance apart so that the flames did not burn him. But he was taken to hospital and his nerve was affected for some considerable time afterwards. But he did eventually recover his nerve and he did a good job during the France/Germany Campaign.

When approaching an ALG (Advanced Landing Ground) the drill was to do so as a bird approaches its nest, taking great care not to reveal to anyone where its nest is. The pilot would approach the field, threading his way through any trees, and then reduce his flying speed by raising the nose of the aircraft. As the aircraft began to sink, he would control its sink by skilful use of the throttle. The higher the nose of the aircraft, the more throttle would be required, and the shorter would be the landing. When the wheels were just above the beginning of the landing strip, he would cut the throttle and the aircraft would sink on to the ground without any preliminary float. Where, as was usually the case, there was a cross-wind, the pilot when approaching his landing strip did a flat turn so that his drift over the ground was leading straight down the centre of the strip. Then, as he landed, he had to apply rudder and brakes so as to get the aircraft to run straight down the strip.

Of course it was not as simple as this. It required immense skill and long experience, and a thorough knowledge of all the wind 'gremlins' that one was likely to encounter on that particular day and on that particular strip. When we were instructors we used to lecture on all the 'gremlins' which we had to be prepared to meet.

The only instruments with which our aircraft were then fitted were a 'rev counter', a compass which required 'swinging' far more often that it was in fact swung, a turn and bank indicator (which was useless when flying in cloud), and an airspeed indicator which was often very inaccurate when the rubber band round the pitot head had shifted or come off altogether. So the necessary cockpit checks before take-off and before landing did not take very long. Flaps and altimeters came later.

But when we got the Vigilant we had to remember to check 'Trim Mixture Pitch Fuel Flaps Gills' before take-off, and 'Pitch Mixture Flaps Trim' before landing. If we had ever forgotten one of these, disaster might have resulted. John Ingram solved this problem for us by inventing two phrases designed to ensure that we remembered everything. They were 'Tickle Mary Pickford Fee Five Guineas' before take-off, and 'Poke Mary For Tuppence' before landing.

Before our Second Course Charles Bazeley had doffed his blue uniform and returned to the Army. We did not see him until he reappeared as a major in brown and took command of 651 Squadron just before Exercise Bumper, though he did not actually come with us on Bumper.

S/Ldr Roddy Davenport gave us instruction in flying, most of which was in choosing fields and short landings. The six of us on the course, when out flying without Roddy, Ralph or Jim to control us, held a competition as to who could stop the quickest after landing over a barbed wire fence. Evelyn of course won after hitting the fence with his tailskid. Such competitions are not good ideas.

Later on, Montagu (always known as 'Monty') designed and fitted a contrivance whereby we could switch the wireless set behind us in the aircraft from send to receive, or vice versa, simply by pressing a 'tit' at the top of the joystick.

CHAPTER VII

Early Days of 651 AOP Squadron RAF

In August 1941, 651 Squadron was formed and about a month later we were equipped with Taylorcraft aircraft which had been fitted with Lycoming engines which were entirely inadequate for the purpose for which they were intended. In order to start them, the 'prop' was moved with one finger until it came to the only cylinder on which there was any compression. Then, after a vigorous swing, the engine might possibly be persuaded to start. The take-off run was very long and the subsequent rate of climb was negligible. It would have been quite reasonable of us if we had refused to operate with them but we were then in no position to be fussy.

We were equipped with RAF two-wheel drive vehicles which had been designed for use on RAF stations and were quite unfit to be driven across wet grass fields. The only vehicles provided for pilots when they had to travel on the ground were motorcycles with sidecars. As these sidecars were designed for short men only when the roof was down, I usually rode the motorcycle and found that, as it was leaning towards the sidecar, it was extremely difficult to turn to the right. The men were all RAF personnel and they disapproved intensely of our aircraft (so did we), of us (referring to us as 'brown jobs') and of ever having to spend a night away from the comforts of an RAF station. In short, their morale was very low. We had a few days in which to teach them map reading and to take part with them in a few short exercises. Then the entire Squadron went up to Halstead and on the 29th of September 1941 we began Exercise Bumper. This was undoubtedly the most important exercise in Air OP history. We had to prove to the Army that we were capable of doing the job for which we had been formed. Failure in this would have meant the end of the Air OP. Our Corps Commander, Lt-General Massy, had been one of Charles Bazeley's early supporters and he visited us the day before the Exercise began and wished us luck. By that time Ralph and I were getting on together reasonably well, but I was glad that I was to be in Jim Neathercoat's Flight.

The night before the Exercise began, all the officers of the Squadron dined together in a pub in Halstead. Ralph made a very good light-hearted speech after dinner. We were all in jovial mood though few of us expected to survive the exercise. Torrential rain fell all through that night. Our aircraft were parked on an enormous stubble field nearby and we then had no covers to put on them. It occurred to us that they would be very difficult to start. They had of course been picketed down.

Monkey Morgan and I slept on the floor of the pub lounge. We slept in our clothes as all our kit and bedding was in the trucks in which our ground crews were moving along the road from Clare to Luton. We had kept with us only our shaving and washing things as we didn't want to carry any more weight in the aircraft than was absolutely necessary. It was unfortunate that we would have to carry our aircraft pickets with us. The RAF issue of iron folding chocks were far too heavy to carry in the aircraft and throughout the War we put our gas masks in front of one wheel and our 'tin hats' in front of the other. We were supposed to carry these two items with us always and so we used them in this way.

Monkey and I got up just before dawn. We found the field so waterlogged that we only just succeeded in getting our aircraft off the ground. After take-off I found that my aircraft wallowed about and refused to climb. I had some near misses with trees and I then noticed that water was pouring out of the mainplanes and then down the perspex of the cockpit obscuring my view. Obviously the wings had become completely waterlogged during the night. Gradually the aircraft became lighter and I was then able to climb, fly to the road which was the axis of the advance of 54 Div and then look for my ground party. It was still raining.

The road was packed with Army vehicles each of which had to keep the appropriate distance from the vehicle in front and they all had to keep moving. I flew eleven sorties that day and from time to time my aircraft had to be refuelled. This presented a problem as vehicles were not permitted to stop on the road and my RAF 30-cwt truck got bogged down as soon as it got on grass. It was necessary for me to try to keep in step with the gunner regiment for which I was going to observe – otherwise I might have flown over the 'enemy'. This meant that I had to land every few miles in fields beside the road and suitable fields were not easy to find. I remember particularly two of the fields which I used.

The first was a narrow and fairly long field which sloped down to a village through which the road ran. The slope was very slight near the village but became increasingly steep as one went up the hill. The wind was only slight and so I decided to land downwind and up the hill. I thought I would then be able to taxi to the top of the hill and take off into the slight wind and down the long hill. I landed without difficulty and the aircraft came to an abrupt halt in the boggy ground. As I waited for my gunner regiment to catch up with me, I wondered whether or not I would be able to get my aircraft up to the top of the hill.

I held the joystick into my tummy and opened to full throttle and managed to persuade the aircraft to move halfway up the hill, but there it stuck. Meanwhile the entire village had come out to watch my efforts. So I asked some of them to assist me and I showed them where to push on the wing struts. With their assistance I eventually managed to taxi to a place further up the slope from which I believed that I would be able to take off.

I had got out of the aircraft in order to show the villagers where to push and this had resulted in my Army boots becoming caked in thick mud. As I climbed back into the cockpit a dear old lady insisted on peeling off with her hands the mud from my boots. It was a kind act which I will never forget. In that mud I doubted that I would ever be able to get the aircraft off the ground, but I felt that I had to have a go.

I opened to full throttle and the aircraft began to move slowly down the hill skidding as it went. I pulled the stick back in order to take as much weight as possible off the wheels and then slowly edged it forward as the aircraft approached flying speed. Finally it got off the ground and I went between two houses and very narrowly missed some telephone cables.

The other problem field in which I landed that day had a reasonably good grass surface but was rather small. After I had landed, it seemed a bit too small and, as it was surrounded by low trees, I decided that it was unlikely that I would get out of it again. I taxied to the hedge beside the road and switched off. Then I paced the field again and again, considered the wind and the height of the trees and eventually decided that I might just make it if only I could first jettison the wireless set and all unnecessary weight such as the aircraft pickets, my tin hat, gas mask and greatcoat. So I waited beside the road with all these things until the convoy halted for a few moments and then I hurriedly asked someone who was sitting in the back of a truck if he would kindly take my surplus luggage, saying that I would collect them from him again as soon as I had found a larger field further down the road.

Unfortunately the junior officer to whom I had spoken was very security-minded and he demanded to see my identity card. As I handed it to him his truck moved on, leaving me without an identity card, which was a bad thing at any time and very bad during an Army exercise. Fortunately a few minutes later a cousin of mine, Aidan Briggs, who was in the 86th Field Regiment RA to which I was then attached, came along the road, stopped for a moment at my urgent request, took my luggage on board and undertook the job of recovering my identity card for me. I just got out of that field, though I think my wheels brushed through the top of a tree.

I think every other pilot of 651 Squadron had similar or worse experiences that day. Some took off under telephone wires and some went through them. Some, including Jim Neathercoat, turned upside-down in the mud. Monkey Morgan flew into HT cables and was taken to hospital very severely injured. I didn't see him again until after the War.

That night was wet and cold. I slept in a wet ditch with the 86th Field Regiment: my ground crew slept in their truck. The following day I did about a dozen 'dummy' shoots and when I finally landed just before sunset, I found that my ground crew had left and driven away to an unknown destination. I subsequently learned that they had had enough of working with the Army and had gone in search of the comforts of an RAF station. They had left me without any petrol or servicing facilities, without a groundsheet, blankets or greatcoat. In fact I had only my shaving things and toothbrush. The obvious thing for me to do was to fly to the nearest RAF station myself where I would spend the night in comfort and where my aircraft would be serviced. I therefore set off for Debden.

It was an ambition of most Air OP pilots during the War to find an ALG in a park or field which adjoined a lovely country house in which there lived a beautiful daughter. That evening, when I was on my way to Debden, I saw below me a large and attractive country house with lovely garden and a suitable adjoining field. It occurred to me that the house was large enough for a considerable family of daughters. So I decided to find out whether or not the occupants would be willing to put me up for the night. There was very little wind and the aircraft would not need to be picketed down. I landed, taxied up to a fence, switched off and walked round an enormous clump of rhododendron bushes and into the garden.

I was wearing a dirty old raincoat and my Army boots were covered with mud. I wore no hat, and as I had been wearing a flying helmet which was attached to the wireless set, my hair was probably rather ruffled. But it never occurred to me that I was looking like a tramp.

As I walked hesitantly across the garden towards the house, a man came to meet me. I assumed that he must be the owner. I did not like to ask him straight away whether he would put me up for the night and so I said simply, 'I have just landed an aircraft the other side of those rhododendrons. Could you please tell me where I am?' I did not like saying this. I knew perfectly well where I was and in any event no Air OP pilot ever liked admitting that he didn't know where he was. But I couldn't think of anything else to say. He looked at me in a strange way and remained silent. So I repeated my question. He replied, 'If you have landed an aircraft the other side of those rhododendron bushes, you've come to the right place. This is the —— lunatic asylum. I am the medical superintendent.'

I decided that it was time for me to return to my aircraft and he followed me with evident suspicion. But when he saw the aircraft he apologized for having mistaken me for one of the inmates. He said that he had been in the RFC during the First World War and so I got him to swing my prop for me. I landed at Debden after dark by the light coming from hangar doors which had been left open in breach of the blackout regulations.

Exercise Bumper lasted for two more days and Geoffrey Pollitt and I refuelled at either

31

Debden or Luton and stayed a night at each. Geoffrey also had been deserted by his ground party: in fact most of us were so deserted. This suggested that before the exercise began these RAF ground crews had decided together that, if they should have to sleep out, they would exercise their 'rights' and drive to an RAF station. They even used to talk about 'government time' and their 'own time'.

Charles Bazeley thought of having these bloody-minded ground crews court-martialled but he quite rightly decided that this would only cause trouble between the two services. The lessons taught by Exercise Bumper were that both the Lycoming engine and the RAF vehicles were totally inadequate for the job and that we must have ground crews who were both willing and loyal. We continued throughout the War to have RAF personnel to maintain and repair the aircraft but in due course we were equipped with Army four-wheel drive vehicles and an Air OP Squadron became an excellent mixture of RAF and Army personnel whose loyalty was to the Air OP.

After Exercise Bumper we had three days at Old Sarum in which to prepare for the next exercise. This was to be Exercise Percy which was to be held in the neighbourhood of Hexham in Northumberland. Only one Flight was to take part in this exercise. Tetley Tetley-Jones was to be the flight commander and Bill Ballard (who was later killed when a squadron commander, practising evasive tactics), Bob Harker, Evelyn Prendergast and I were to be the section officers. As the Lycoming engine had proved such a disaster, we persuaded Roddy Davenport to lend us, for the exercise, training aircraft from Larkhill. On the 7th of October 1941, Tetley sent us off separately from Old Sarum with instructions to spend that night at York and to be at an ALG next to Catterick racecourse the following day. None of us got to York that day.

I set off in a Taylorcraft fitted with a Cirrus engine. It was also fitted with a sensitive altimeter which could be relied on if one set it correctly. This aircraft had one disadvantage: the rubber band round the pitot head kept on shifting, with the result that one had to guess one's speed.

Visibility was moderate and there was little wind. The Thames Valley was covered by a thick mist, but flying at about 1,000 feet I went over the top and soon saw the ground again. I refuelled at Thame and later at Grantham. After leaving Grantham I flew under a thick dark cloud only a few hundred feet above the ground and as this cloud got lower and lower as I went north, I decided to follow the railway line so as to avoid getting lost. Before long I found that, whenever I pulled up in order to get over HT cables or trees, I went into cloud and temporarily lost sight of the ground. This was when I should have turned back to Grantham.

We were all Army pilots with Army ideas. The Army does not turn back just because the weather is too bad. If our Flight was committed to take part in an Army exercise, the new idea of an Air OP would be discredited if we failed to turn up and gave the weather as our excuse. We were claiming that we flew even if 'the birds were walking'. So I was determined to get through to York somehow.

Our aircraft were not equipped for flying in cloud. My only instruments were a turn and bank indicator, an altimeter and an inaccurate airspeed indicator. I had no artificial horizon and this is essential for cloud flying. Our wireless communication was very local and only to Army ground sets and on a cross-country flight we had no communication whatever with the ground. In fact we flew as the pilots of the First World War had flown – by our bottoms which told us when we were skidding or slipping or near to a stall. But though an experienced pilot's bottom will tell him when things have gone wrong when cloud flying, only an artificial horizon will tell him how to put them right again.

So as I pulled up into that cloud that day I knew that if things went wrong I had 'had it'. I resolved to centralize the stick and rudder, ignore the turn and bank indicator if it should go haywire, concentrate on both the airspeed indicator and my sense of the climbing speed and rely on the natural stability of the aircraft. When flying in dense cloud one is apt to suspect that one may be upside-down, but I ignored the bumps caused by the cloud and the aircraft did not fail me. At 2,000 feet I emerged into brilliant sunlight and I then flew along the top of the cloud until my navigational calculations told me that I was approaching York. I adjusted my altimeter according to the respective heights above sea-level of Grantham and York and then started to descend through the cloud in the same manner as I had come up through it. I don't think it had then occurred to me that there might be dense fog in York.

I intended to descend until I got below the cloud and then try to find the aerodrome at York. But when my altimeter registered only 70 feet I reluctantly opened the throttle and pulled up again. I flew above the cloud on a reverse course until I estimated that I was some-where near Grantham and then went down through the cloud again and fortunately found that the cloud base there was about 200 feet. I refuelled again at Grantham and then flew north beside the railway line and under the cloud as far as Finningley. When I landed there the fog was so dense that I had considerable difficulty in finding my way to the hangars. In fact someone came out and escorted me in. Someone else gave me a rocket: the RAF did not expect anyone to fly in such conditions. I learned when I arrived in York the following day that visibility there had been only five yards. I wonder whether I had narrowly missed some-one's roof in York.

Perhaps I should add that we usually obtained a route forecast before we took off from an RAF airfield, but we did not allow any such forecast to discourage us from taking off pro-vided that there was no gale warning and visibility was adequate when we did so. As I have said, the Army didn't stop fighting just because visibility was poor.

I have told this story at some length because it illustrates one of our greatest problems at that time. If we ran into low cloud resulting in mist or fog, we could either turn back, or get down somewhere, or make for the nearest RAF aerodrome ahead. Turning back might not help if the cloud was getting lower everywhere. Picking a field and landing in it was to be avoided if possible. Quite apart from the fact that cattle and horses are apt to damage aircraft, we could not just leave an aircraft in a field unguarded and a fog might last for days. So in practice we went on until we reached the nearest comfortable RAF station. The RAF, despite our brown uniforms and then lack of wings, would always welcome us. There were no smokeless zones in those days and we learned in due course that the Midlands of England were shrouded in mist during most of the winter and we also learned which aerodromes were the most comfortable places at which to become fog-bound. Rearsby, where our Austers were built, became a great favourite, because they always welcomed us, looked after our air-craft and provided us with transport into Leicester where we stayed at an excellent hotel. Shows destined for London were first tried out at the theatre in Leicester. Montagu and I once became fog-bound there and saw the play *While the Sun Shines* and met the cast (Jane Baxter, Michael Standing and Hugh MacDermott) who were also staying at our hotel.

I was about to say that I learned by my mistake when I was flying to York in October 1941, that when continuous cloud comes down to the ground we should never fly up through it and hope to get down again somewhere else. But, now that I come to think of it, I made an even more stupid mistake a year or so later when I was a flying instructor at Larkhill. My then commanding officer Donald Walker (who was later shot down and killed when flying a Mosquito) had detailed me to give a lecture on the Air OP to a Senior Officers' Conference (composed of generals and air marshals) at Old Sarum. Donald had offered me ground transport to take me there, but I had refused this as the sun was shining through a thick white ground mist and I was quite certain that the mist would have cleared before I was due to take off. The lecture was fixed for 1030 hrs and the flight there would only take a few minutes.

At 1015 hrs I was waiting in an aircraft ready to take off. I could see the sun shining through the mist and I unwisely assumed that when I got above it I would be able to see the ground. At any rate it was too late for me to go by road and it was unthinkable that I, a mere captain, should keep generals and air marshals waiting. So I took off and hoped for the best.

At about 200 feet I emerged into brilliant sunlight and for as far as I could see in every direction there was a continuous cloud, like shining white cotton wool, beneath me. I set course for Old Sarum, but when I got there I could only see the tip of the spire of Salisbury Cathedral. I flew round it for a few minutes and then I saw vaguely through the mist the tops of the hangars at Old Sarum. I knew this airfield and so I was able to judge where it would be safe for me to land. I set the aircraft for a blind short landing through the mist and as soon as I felt the wheels touch the ground I cut the throttle. The mist was much thicker than it had been at Larkhill and I could see nothing at all as I landed or after I had done so. An indignant Duty Pilot came out to me and led me in the direction of the Watch Office where I switched off. He began to say what he thought of my flying in such weather conditions but I ran to the lecture room and arrived there only two minutes late which no one appeared to notice.

But I have digressed and followed my thoughts. Exercise Percy was a great success so far as the Air OP were concerned. Tetley was a very efficient flight commander and we broke no aircraft. We much enjoyed flying over the very attractive Northumberland countryside. The exercise lasted for four days and I see from my log book that I did about a dozen sorties each day, taking off before dawn and landing finally at dusk. I did 'dummy shoots' for 10th Field Regiment, 76th Medium Regiment and 6th RHA and I did sorties to watch the progress of the 9th Armoured Division. I doubt that it then occurred to anyone that one day an Air OP job would be to fly ahead of our leading tanks in Germany and report by R/T on whether or not white flags had been put out by each German village.

But my most vivid memory of Exercise Percy was sleeping one night in a large haystack beside the Flight ALG. I say 'sleeping' but I don't think I slept much that night. Throughout the night I listened to the rustling sound of rats moving about the hay. When they got near me they paused and then slowly walked round me. If I had not been able to hear them so clearly I would probably not have minded. As it was, it was very difficult not to lie awake and listen to them.

By this time our RAF ground personnel were beginning to get to know us and to think that working with the Army was not so bad after all. After the Exercise we had a party at Catterick aerodrome and then Evelyn Prendergast and I were detailed to take one Piper Cub and one ground party up to Otterburn Ranges to do some live shoots with 2nd Field Regiment. We made our base at Woolsington Aerodrome, near Newcastle and flew up to an ALG near the Ranges each day. We decided that both we and our ground party would prefer to stay at a comfortable aerodrome rather than to sleep in a field beside the Ranges at the end of October. The ground party made quite a lot of pocket-money by gathering mushrooms on or near our ALG and selling them in Newcastle in the evenings.

Our first day at Otterburn was nearly our last. We established a suitable ALG without any difficulty but then a strong wind got up and it rained in torrents. I went by road to the house beside the road to Carter Bar where we were to be given our orders for the shoots and Evelyn said that he would try to find somewhere to land near it. He in fact landed on a tiny area of grass and rushes surrounded by a bog and in the shelter of a line of trees. It was just the other side of the road from the house where some senior gunner officers and I were and we watched his landing. This must have convinced the gunner officers that the Air OP could land just about anywhere. But I knew that, if there had not been almost a gale, he could not have landed there and I doubted that he could possibly take off again. The wind was so strong that the Piper Cub was in danger of being blown over when stationary on the ground. Evelyn's approach to land had been so slow that the aircraft had stopped as soon as the wheels had touched the ground and the throttle was cut. It was clear that it would take off again as soon as he opened to full throttle but the question that was worrying both of us was what would happen when it reached the shelter of the line of trees.

On such occasions the drill is to climb as steeply as possible immediately after take-off and to try in this way to keep in the wind. If one gets into the shelter of trees, the flying speed is lost and down comes the aircraft so that it crashes into the trees. Evelyn was briefed for a live shoot, succeeded in getting over, or through, the trees, and then began the shoot while I returned by road to our ALG.

He joined me there a few minutes later. He had had to break off a shoot because a low cloud had swept over us, covering all the hills in a thick mist. Two alternatives were then open to us: we could either picket the aircraft down and spend an extremely uncomfortable night on the ALG, or we could send off our ground crew in the truck and ourselves attempt to fly back to the comforts of Woolsington. We decided on the latter course. It was my turn to fly the aircraft, and Evelyn offered to map read for me.

The aircraft took off almost as soon as I opened to full throttle and we flew across a valley towards hills which were shrouded in thick mist. We found a railway line (now disused) and wisely decided to follow that. As we entered the mist I kept a few feet above the rails, realizing that I must not under any circumstances lose sight of them – or we would have 'had it'. I asked Evelyn to make sure that the railway line did not go under a tunnel and he replied that he couldn't see one marked on the map. We joked about the possibility of colliding head-on with a train.

After what seemed an age we were across the hills and down the other side and then we were able to fly at a height of over 50 feet which meant that we should be safe from telephone wires and bridges. He told me that we were approaching a road bridge over our railway line and that I should there turn right and follow the road towards Newcastle. The mist grew darker as we approached Newcastle and we would have missed Woolsington Aerodrome if the Duty Pilot had not heard us and fired off a number of Very cartridges so as to show us where the aerodrome was. We received the usual rocket for flying in such weather conditions, but we were glad that we had done so. We went to a theatre in Newcastle that evening.

The remainder of our visit to Otterburn was fairly uneventful. The wind continued strong but no more low clouds covered the hills while we were flying. We each did quite a number of live shoots, hiding behind hills from the imaginary enemy and only climbing up for a few moments in order to observe the fall of shot. Frequently a shell landed with a splash in a peat bog and did not explode. Those ranges are probably still full of unexploded shells.

Before I leave the subject of low cloud appearing suddenly and covering hills in mist, I will follow my thoughts and write of an occasion in December 1943 when my Squadron were doing live shoots on some ranges near Pickering in Yorkshire. These were the Saltergate Ranges just north of Pickering.

We were all billeted in Pickering – I had a feather bed which was hell. Monty was instructing the men in the firing of a Bren gun and just after he had told them that the Bren, when fixed to fire single rounds was a fairly accurate weapon, he saw a blackcock standing on a boulder a considerable distance away. As it was the 6th of December, the blackcock were still in season but he was of course poaching. He killed that blackcock with a single shot. That evening he presented it to the lady of the house where he was billeted. A few minutes later her daughter came back from work – she was in the uniform of a police sergeant but did not raise the matter of poaching.

That day we were doing shoots with the 150th Field Regiment. I decided to experiment with 'visual shoots'. These shoots assumed that the pilot's wireless set had been put out of action by enemy fire – this in fact happened all too often during the France / Germany Campaign. The pilot then dropped a message bag explaining that he was about to do a visual shoot and giving the map reference of the target. Corrections were given as follows: climbing meant add, diving meant drop, and side-slipping meant corrections to line. Then, once ranging had been completed, the number of rounds of gunfire required was shown by the number of complete circles of steep turns done. It was like a game.

I decided that I would myself give a demonstration of how it should be done. All went perfectly until I was doing those four very tight turns. I was very rough with the Auster III so as not to waste time. The clouds were low and I was flying at about 250 feet. After completing three-and-a-half very tight turns I found that the joystick had suddenly gone completely slack – I had stalled the aircraft. I instantly took the necessary action and so got out of trouble and didn't go into a spin. But after that I was not so keen on visual shoots.

In another shoot that day one pilot dropped a 25-pounder shell among a group of sheep. One was killed but the others did not even appear to be hurt. This made us a bit sceptical about the killing power of 25-pounder shells. I sent an officer (probably Monty) to apologise profusely to the farmer and to give him a certificate which would enable him to claim compensation. The farmer's wife mentioned that their only wireless set had not worked since the beginning of the War and they couldn't get it repaired. Our establishment included several wireless experts and so I sent one of them to repair the set.

Towards the end of that day, after just about every pilot had done at least one shoot, Nelson, who had been attached to us as a supernumerary pilot for training, was up doing a shoot when a thin low cloud came up from behind us and we suddenly found that visibility had become practically nil.

The correct drill on such occasions was to fly downwind until one could see the ground again and then land somewhere. But perhaps I had not explained the correct drill to Nelson. At any rate he decided to do a short landing somewhere near our ALG and hope for the best. He came down through the fog and was lucky in that he touched down on fairly level grass and in an open space. But, being unable to see what was in front of him, he braked much too violently and his aircraft came to rest upside-down. Fortunately he had cut the switches as soon as he landed and the only damage to the aircraft was a broken prop which was replaced within a few minutes. He was quite unhurt.

Nelson was an excellent chap and I wished that I had been able to keep him in my Squadron. But shortly after that he was posted away, I think to the Far East. I do hope he survived the War.

CHAPTER VIII

The Isle of Wight

On the 12th of November 1941, Tetley sent me to the Isle of Wight to replace Bob Harker who had just crashed there. Bob was very seriously injured and was never again fit for flying duties. The trouble was that the Lycoming engine had not enough power for the job. We had had to return the 'D' Flight aircraft which we had borrowed for Exercise Percy.

My orders were to fly to the Fleet Air Arm aerodrome at Worthy Down and there obtain instructions as to the route which I must follow in order to get to Bob's ALG at Ryde. Both Southampton and Portsmouth were surrounded by balloon barrages and the South Coast abounded in anti-aircraft crews who might be a bit too quick on the trigger.

My flight to Ryde was uneventful, but I found that Bob's ALG was a football field surrounded by trees and with some terrible ridges which must have made it as unsuitable for football as it was for an ALG. I soon moved to a new ALG just outside Ryde and the ground crew were billeted in a farmhouse which adjoined the field so that they could keep an eye on the aircraft and also ensure that no cattle were allowed in the field during the fortnight that we were there.

I got on very well with that ground crew and they served me well. One of them had played football for Arsenal before the War and so every regiment to which I was attached conveniently forgot that he was Royal Air Force, welcomed him with open arms and persuaded him to play football for them. The rest of us enjoyed his reflected glory. About two years later I met him at an operational bomber station: he had become an air gunner.

As the prevailing wind was from a southerly direction, I habitually found that I either had to take off into wind uphill and hope to get up enough flying speed in order to be able to turn before I flew into a hillside which was becoming steeper as I progressed, or I had to take off downwind downhill and hope to get off the ground before reaching a fence. I did the latter twice and frightened myself so much that I did not try it again. That Lycoming engine could not cope with downwind take-offs.

Each day we took part in exercises with the various troops of the regiment to which I was attached and I see from my log book that I did a great deal of flying then, mostly in sorties of about ten minutes' duration. I learned that ploughmen had an annoying habit of putting up long sticks in stubble fields in order to assist them in ploughing straight furrows. They were probably annoyed by my habit of taking these sticks down: I did not want to hit one with my prop. I remember two of the many fields which I used in the Isle of Wight very vividly.

In one of these there were far too many cows for my liking and, as it seemed to be nearly always raining, their cowpats were of a very liquid variety. As a result, before I got that wretched aircraft off the ground my forward vision was entirely obscured by cowpats. So I landed in the next field which was smaller but free from cows and there I cleaned the perspex as best I could. All I had for that purpose was my handkerchief and it was entirely inadequate, but it was vital that I should be able to see. When I took off again in that sodden ground, this next field proved to be too small and, though I just persuaded that aircraft to jump the fence, it sagged into the other field and collected a few more cowpats.

The other field which I particularly remember was a grass field without cows somewhere on the south-east coast of the island and one side was a high cliff with the sea below. After I had successfully landed there, I paced this field again and again, considered the wind very carefully and wondered whether or not my aircraft would reach flying speed before it went over the cliff, and, if it didn't, whether it would reach flying speed before it got to the rocks below. Fortunately I never learned the answer to the second question.

When it was growing dark one evening a small Boy Scout arrived on my ALG and demanded to know whether my aircraft had been properly immobilised. All unattended vehicles had to be immobilised in those days by removing the rotor arm of the distributor. The aircraft had already been picketed down for the night in the shelter of some trees and the covers had been put on.

That aircraft was such a brute to start every morning that I merely assured the Boy Scout that no enemy spy or escaped prisoner of war would ever succeed in starting it and that, even if he did, he would never get it out of that field after dark. This did not satisfy that Boy Scout and he wanted to know why there was no guard on the aircraft all night. This was a tricky question as, according to RAF regulations, there should have been a guard, but one cannot mount a guard by night with only four men who have to work hard all day. This was always a problem when Air OP sections were operating separately. So I asked the boy to let me know if ever he saw any suspicious characters in the neighbourhood and he thus became the unofficial guard.

One day I had toothache and as my dentist of before the War had joined the Navy and was stationed at Worthy Down, I decided to visit him there. I flew to Cowes where I was told what route to follow and they said that the balloons along this route through Southampton would be 'close hauled' between certain hours. They omitted to tell me that 'close hauled' meant hauled down to 1,000 feet and I assumed that it meant that they would all be hauled down to the ground. As I was flying at about 200 feet on the right side of the main road from Portsmouth to Southampton, I suddenly noticed the balloons above me. So I got down even lower and kept in the centre of the main road. I noticed one vehicle to which a balloon was attached parked beside the road, but saw it in time to avoid the cable.

When I was about to take off from Worthy Down a sailor stopped me and said that the 'Commander Flying' wanted to see me: he added that the Commander wanted to know who had authorized my flight. So I taxied back, switched off and reported to the Commander and assured him that I was entitled to authorize my own flights. He did not believe me at first but he accepted my argument that as I was the only pilot with an aircraft in the Isle of Wight and as I had just flown in from there, I must be entitled to authorize my own flights.

He then changed his tack and said, 'If I were to land at a strange airfield and someone were to offer to authorize my flight, I would consider it courteous to accept his offer.' Being then unversed in the ways of the Senior Service, I entirely missed the hint which he had given me and stupidly apologized for having 'Hurt his feelings'. This led to an outburst of his wrath. His final words to me were, 'I don't care who the hell authorizes your blasted flights.' The flights of Air OP officers were never authorized in any book. But Air OP wings had not yet been approved or even designed and few people had even heard of us.

On the 25th of November 1941, I was to do some live shoots with the Regiment on the Isle of Wight Artillery Range. This was a tiny range and I doubt that it is still used as such. I was briefed as to my target and I then ran to my aircraft, took off and began the shoot. I gave the guns the map reference which I had been given: the target was a clump of bushes in the middle of the Range. The guns reported 'Shot 1', but I saw no burst anywhere on the Range. So I followed the accepted procedure and dropped four hundred yards: again I saw no burst.

So I ordered a slight change of line, but fortunately a ghost voice then came over the air, 'Your last round fell twelve hundred yards south of your target and one hundred yards from an inhabited farmhouse.' The ghost voice was the voice of Tetley who, unknown to me, had just flown over from Old Sarum, had netted in to my wireless frequency and had been watching the shoot from high above me. Thank heaven I had such an excellent flight commander, or there might have been a real disaster.

So I ordered the guns to check their line and they soon found that they were 12 degrees out. Once this had been put right all went well. The Colonel hurried off to make suitable apologies at the inhabited farmhouse and was relieved to find that no actual damage had been done. After I had returned to Old Sarum, Charles Bazeley showed me a report which that Colonel had sent in about me. It was a good report and Charles was evidently pleased with it. But it did end with the sentence, 'Captain Lyell broke no aircraft but he did scare the wits out of a number of sheep.' Well, it wasn't my fault.

CHAPTER IX
Flying Instructors

From the 15th of February until the 8th of April 1942, Evelyn Prendergast and I were on a Flying Instructors' Course at Cambridge. John Ingram and Norman Lane had been on the previous course and Geoffrey Pollitt and Peter Dowse were on the one after us. The Air OP had by then in the opinion of Higher Authority proved itself and the policy now was to train instructors who would train the many Air OP pilots who would in due course be required to provide twelve Air OP operational squadrons and all the necessary supernumeraries and reinforcements. It was, I believe, sometime in the spring of 1942 that we at last got Air OP wings.

By the time that Evelyn and I reported to S/Ldr Roddy Davenport in April 1942, '"D" Flight RAF' had become '1424 Flight'. On the first course after we had become instructors, I was detailed to instruct Eley, Fowler, Skae and Shield. They were all very competent pilots. In fact Skae was quite brilliant and this brilliance perhaps contributed to excessive confidence which may have led to his accident shortly after he joined Ralph Cobley's 652 Squadron. Skae was very severely injured and did not fly again.

On the next course I had Moke Murray (N. J. Murray), John Stormonth-Darling, Vic Cowley and Michael Mates. The first three of these were excellent natural pilots who were a pleasure to teach. But Mates was a problem and if the EFTS had had a clue as to what Air OP pilots had to learn to do they would never have passed him on to us.

Mates became violently sick whenever he did a steep turn and whenever he was being sick, he told me that he could not continue flying the aircraft. I stupidly hoped that he would get over this, and persevered. Trying to teach him how to do short landings was my worst problem. An instructor should not keep his own hands or feet on the controls but should endeavour to instruct by word of mouth only. Doing short landings is a difficult art and required great sensitivity. I was instructing Mates in a DH82 when he suddenly cut the throttle at about 100 feet and the aircraft dropped like a stone. Neither of us was hurt but the aircraft was a complete write-off. I then asked John Ingram, who was at that time the senior Air OP pilot at Larkhill, to give Mates a test. John agreed with me that the only thing to do was to send Mates back to his regiment.

For a time after that my confidence as an instructor was somewhat strained and my pupils on the next course (David Donald, Denny, Price and Tom Bishop) may have felt my hand on the throttle. But I had no more bad pilots and as a result my confidence gradually returned.

Tom Bishop was a problem in other ways. He was a delightful character and everyone liked him. Had it not been for this we would certainly have failed him after he had got a bit lost during his test shoot at the end of the course. Perhaps it would have been kinder if we had failed him, as he got lost in North Africa where he landed behind the German lines and was taken prisoner. Dick Odgers was also taken prisoner there but later escaped and brought back to England the story that the German officer who interrogated him had told him that he had previously interrogated an Air OP officer who, at the end of the interrogation, had shaken

Evelyn Prendergast.

Geoffrey Pollitt.

him warmly by the hand and said, 'After the War you must come and dine with me at the Cavalry Club.' This was just the sort of thing that Tom would have said, but it puzzled that German officer.

Tom once told me of something he had done when flying before the War. He had wondered whether or not a hen could fly. So he took one up to 5,000 feet where he threw it out of the window of the aircraft and then watched its descent. It came down in a tight spiral turn and landed safely.

Whenever any pilot met with an accident a signal had to be made to the Air Ministry and this signal had to be followed as soon as possible by an accident report. The Air Ministry sought to minimize the number of accidents and so from time to time sent rockets to Army Co-op Command which passed them down to Groups and Squadrons. A few days after Roddy Davenport had passed on one of these rockets to us, there were three accidents to pupils in one day. Evelyn and I, when out on the exercise which led to these accidents, were wondering what Roddy would say when we told him of them. In fact all he said was, 'Serves you right for flying on Friday, the 13th.'

My only experience of engine failure was when I was a flying instructor at Larkhill and flying, with a pupil, an ancient pre-war Taylorcraft. Shortly after take-off from a field somewhere on Salisbury Plain smoke came pouring from the engine (an oil pipe had broken). I immediately took over from the pupil, switched off, and made a successful forced landing. Engine failures in the Air OP were very rare until after we landed in Normandy when they became far too frequent. 658 Squadron had no less than three inexplicable engine failures in Normandy – one shortly after take-off (pilot unhurt), one in flight (pilot unhurt though aircraft overturned on forced landing in cornfield), and one when a pilot was taking violent evasive action from a playful Typhoon (engine re-started in flight). And, later on, Ian MacNaughton had an inexplicable engine failure when testing a field to make sure that he would be able to take the Army Commander out of it safely. Ian spent a short time in hospital and his aircraft, which had only been fetched from England a few days before, was destroyed.

Our type of low flying would not really have been dangerous at all had it not been for HT cables. Pilots flew into HT cables far too often. The usual trouble was when the pylons were hidden behind two nearby woods: a pilot flew low through the gap between the two woods and only saw the wires when it was too late to avoid them.

When an aircraft flies into HT cables, much depends on how many cables there are and on how high they are above the ground. Also on what part of the aircraft takes the shock of the impact. One of our pupils at Larkhill, when flying solo in a Taylorcraft, collided with five HT cables. Three of them were cut by the impact, but the other two came down with the aircraft and were still entangled with it on the ground. Fortunately the pilot had the good sense to get out of the wreck as quickly as he possibly could and get away from it. The drill at the power station when fuses were blown was to replace the fuses and then switch on again. That pilot was quite unhurt, though his nerve probably sustained considerable temporary damage.

Pat Henderson was making an unauthorised simulated attack (some people, including Pat, might have described it as 'beating up') on a regiment which was proceeding along the road which runs through the Wylye Valley. He was flying a DH82 and making a concealed approach between two woods when he collided with three HT cables which he had not seen because the wooden pylons were at the edge of each wood. The aircraft cut all three cables, but one of them had sliced through the petrol tank, which in a DH82 is above the pilot's

No. 7 AOP Course at Larkhill, May 1942 (Roddy Davenport was still then in command).

Left to right, standing: Captains Riding, Henderson, Stormonth-Darling, Lieutenants Mates, Billingham, Glover, Tallents, Gulland, Captain Stubbs, Lieutenants Murray and Cowley. Seated: Captain Bishop, Second Lieutenant Loder, Lieutenant Loder, Captain Prendergast, Captain Lane, Squadron Leader Davenport, Captain Ingram, Captain Lyell (the Author), Lieutenants Colmar and Nicholson.

43

head. A spark ignited the petrol and the aircraft crashed in flames beside an ammunition dump.

Pat lost consciousness on impact but recovered in time to unfasten the straps, get away from the flames and save his life. He was wearing a flying helmet, gloves and goggles, but his exposed face sustained third degree burns and he was in hospital for quite a long time. Nevertheless he subsequently recovered his nerve and later became a very distinguished squadron commander with a great deal of operational service. Now, after forty-two years, his facial burns are almost invisible.

I have drawn a distinction between a 'simulated attack' and 'beating up' because this was very important in an accident report. Higher Authority in the Royal Air Force regarded 'beating up' as a court martial offence, which would lead to the pilot's discharge with ignominy – which at that time was regarded as a fate literally far worse than death. While I was an instructor a fighter pilot beat up a column of soldiers on the march at Larkhill. He flew so low that all but one of the column flung themselves flat on their faces on the road. The one who was too proud to do this and remained standing had his head taken off by a wing of the fighter aircraft.

But when I was an instructor at Larkhill I was on several occasions asked by battery commanders to make surprise simulated attacks on their batteries when moving along roads in the vicinity of Salisbury Plain. This was to give their Bren gunners experience and to test their preparedness. It was great fun for me.

Flying into cables is not like flying into a wall – it is more like flying into a net which breaks. I saw a pupil at Larkhill, when returning to our landing strip after doing a live shoot on Salisbury Plain, fly into and cut three telephone wires: the aircraft appeared to have received a sudden check in its speed, but it just struggled on without stalling and very little harm was done.

Knighton Down (the name of the Larkhill Airfield) had, I believe, not been used as an airfield before 'D' Flight adopted it. At some time in its history an Army telephone line had been laid across it and left there. One day when I was taking off in a Taylorcraft the tailskid got caught up in this line. Just as I was about to become airborne I felt a sudden check to my speed, but, as I realized that I could not stop before hitting the boundary fence, I kept on and just got off the ground before the fence. The check to my speed continued and I found that I needed full throttle to keep the aircraft in the air. I looked round and found that I was towing two or three hundred yards of telephone cable. So I went round and landed again, making sure my tow did not become entangled with any HT cables.

One day I experienced what happens when one lands in an aircraft which has the brake on one wheel locked fully on. I was flying a Piper Cub and had noticed nothing unusual on take-off, and so I assume that something happened then to cause this trouble. On landing, the aircraft went round and round in diminishing circles, but fortunately no one else was taking off or landing at the time.

Instructors much enjoyed their low flying when they were flying alone, flying only a few feet above the ground. One day Peter Dowse returned to Knighton Down with a dead rabbit lodged between one wheel and the strut.

We somehow got hold of an ancient Avro, such as I had been trained on when in the Cambridge University Air Squadron. We made a point of only doing gliding approaches and landings in this – it was so easy to fly that one could touch down every time on a 'T' put out. But this was kept for the amusement of instructors only.

In August 1942, we got a Vigilant to test as to whether or not it would be suitable for the

No. 9 AOP Course at Larkhill, May 1942 (Donald Walker had then just taken over command).

Left to right, standing: Lieutenants Vipond, Eldridge, Captain Bray, Lieutenants McNinch, East, Captains Wood, Knight, Laird, Watkinson, Freeland, Lieutenants Pugh, Seaford and Purvis. Seated: Captain Carr, Captain Jenkyns, Captain Pollitt, Captain Lyell (the Author), Squadron Leader Walker, Captain Prendergast, Captain Dowse, Captain Montagu, Captain Wright.

45

Air OP. Of course we were all for it as take-offs and landings in tiny fields were no problem at all for this aircraft. But it would have been a sitting duck to enemy fighters. Geoffrey and I took it up to see how high we could get it to go. We got it up to 17,700 feet – which was a new experience for Air OP pilots.

Then Geoffrey had a bright idea which very nearly cost both of us our lives. He was determined to do an inverted spin, ie a spin in which the pilot is on the outside instead of the inside. This sounded most uncomfortable, but we had heard stories of this having been done during or not long after the First World War. It was probably strictly forbidden, but this did not worry us unduly.

We took a DH82 up to about 10,000 feet, and then Geoffrey, who was in the front seat and therefore officially the pilot, began a loop, straightened out when we were upside-down and when gliding upside-down, put the aircraft into a spin. It did some very strange things but refused to go into an inverted spin. In what proved to be our final attempt the 'stick' became jammed in the left nearside where it had been put to cause the spin: it was an ordinary spin but we lost a great deal of height as each of us thought that the other was hanging on to the stick. By the time we had learned that the stick was in fact jammed, we were down to 3,000 feet. Geoffrey announced that he was 'baling out' and stood up and was about to go over the side. Then I gave the stick a tremendous blow with my left arm: this centralized the stick and the aircraft's natural stability brought it out of the spin. Thereafter there was no aileron control but otherwise the controls were adequate.

After landing we asked the riggers to strip off the canvas of the port mainplane: they found that a spanner had been left in it at a previous overhaul. It was clearly a case of 'a spanner in the works'.

At about that time British fighter aircraft were fitted with twelve machine-guns. This was not only for shooting down enemy aircraft but also for attacking enemy infantry and non-armoured vehicles on the march on roads. A demonstration of this new firepower of fighter aircraft was arranged to take place on Salisbury Plain in the presence of a considerable gathering of senior Army officers including a number of generals. Monty was then an instructor at Larkhill in technical subjects such as wireless sets and these subjects included firepower of fighter aircraft. So he was detailed to go and observe this demonstration.

A long straight line of dummy soldiers and ancient vehicles was set up to represent a column on the march and the line of the spectators was kept over a hundred yards away from the target. The fighter aircraft were to come in low and knock hell out of the dummy soldiers and ancient vehicles. But someone blundered: perhaps the RAF were unaware of the Army adage that time spent on reconnaissance is seldom wasted. At any rate the leading fighter came in very low, mistook the line of spectators for his target and caused havoc among the senior Army officers – twenty of whom were killed and about seventy seriously wounded. Red Very lights were then fired and these stopped the other fighters from killing the remaining spectators. Monty was among the wounded – he received a bullet or bullets through his thigh.

In the War such major disasters could be hushed up: I do not remember any publicity. Monty has told me that the date of this event was the 13th of April 1942, that he was taken first to a hospital in Bath, then to a hospital in Oxford and finally to Torquay to convalesce. Incidentally at Oxford he was treated by a rather special pre-war friend of mine, the gorgeous Daphne Banks, who had during the War become a physiotherapist. It was not until the middle of November that he was able to return to us and by that time we had become the 43rd OTU at Old Sarum.

On a training exercise on Salisbury Plain. 'Curly' Wood is on the left, the Author is on the right.

'Monty' on an exercise when we were using DH82s.

The Vigilant had a flimsy and very inadequate cap to its petrol tank. One day when I was flying one over the suburbs of Birmingham, I suddenly noticed an intense smell of petrol. I looked round and saw that the cap had come of the petrol tank and was hanging by its chain. It was a very 'bumpy' day and the petrol was being splashed out of the tank and the fuselage was soaked in it. It occurred to me that a single spark from the exhaust would be likely to set the aircraft ablaze. So I throttled only half back, put down full flaps and selected a small paddock in which to land. I descended slowly and in some trepidation, but landed safely. After replacing the cap on the petrol tank, I waited some time for the aircraft to dry out before I took off again.

A senior Army officer (either a brigadier or a colonel) who had had some civilian flying experience before the War, wanted Air OP wings both to decorate his uniform and to assist his Army career by giving him an aura of expertise in all matters pertaining to Army flying. He somehow pulled strings in high places and then came down to us at Larkhill to qualify for obtaining our Air OP wings. Roddy himself took him up to ensure that he would be able to land the aircraft safely on the airfield, though there was of course no prospect at all of teaching him how to do a short landing or correct Air OP flying during a live shoot. We thought this typical of the absurd belief held in high places that Air OP flying was easy.

He was then handed over to us to provide him with the shoot which would, in his exceptional case, qualify him for his wings. That shoot was a complete farce. First he got lost. When he did reappear on the scene he was far too busy flying the aircraft to observe any of the bursts of the ranging shells. The only remaining clump of trees on the Larkhill Artillery Ranges was known as Bunty's Folly and this clump had been preserved by the rule that anyone who dropped a round there had to pay a heavy fine. But our orders were that we must award him his wings somehow and so we gave him Bunty's Folly as his target. No one could possibly miss seeing a shell burst there. Needless to say he got his wings and we did not ask him to pay any fine. But if he subsequently imagined that he had acquired some knowledge of Air OP flying, then I can only say that a little knowledge is a dangerous thing.

CHAPTER X

No.43 Officers' Training Unit

In June 1942, Roddy Davenport left us and went as a wing commander to command a squadron of light bombers. We were very sorry to see him go. His replacement at 1424 Flight was S/Ldr Donald Walker. Donald was not a good pilot and though I showed him how to do a short landing, he never attempted to do any such thing. He did not think it necessary to learn our kind of flying and in this he was probably wise. He was willing to listen to our advice and to take it. So we all got along very well together, and we liked him a lot.

In October 1942, 1424 Flight became 43rd OTU and we moved to Old Sarum. The Air OP was growing fast. Donald became a wing commander and I became a major as CGI (Chief Ground Instructor). Evelyn should obviously have also become a major as CFI (Chief Flying Instructor), but the Air Ministry insisted on this post being filled by an RAF squadron leader. This was every bit as absurd as it would have been if Evelyn or I had been appointed as CFI at a fighter or bomber training school. In fact we could have become expert fighter pilots far more easily than an RAF-trained pilot could learn our job. But though the Air Ministry had not been successful in strangling the Air OP at birth, it was still obviously quite determined that we should never become so independent of the RAF that we might get ideas of becoming part of an Army Air Corps. Though we grumbled at the Air Ministry, we were very happy with the RAF, and if ever we expressed a wish that we were part of an Army Air Corps we did so with the reservation similar to that in St Augustine's famous prayer, 'God give me the strength to lead a chaste life – but not yet.'

Donald Walker was as willing as we were to bend the rules upon occasion. For example, when his pet whippet required exercise, he would take it flying with him, land somewhere on Salisbury Plain and give it a chase after hares.

The RAF sent S/Ldr Hazell to us as CFI: they could not have made a better choice. He was so popular that no one resented the fact that he was a 'blue job'. Old Sarum was a very happy place for all of us. It seemed to be teeming with new Air OP pilots. At first I feared that as CGI my flying would become restricted, but I soon found that this only involved my giving lectures to the pupils in the mornings and during the rest of the day I could give flying instruction, do demonstration shoots at Larkhill and fly any of the various aircraft that happened to be at Old Sarum.

Donald and I were each allotted WAAF Secretaries, though there was very little work for them to do. One of them was beautiful and adorable and so of course Donald chose her for himself. I later learned that she had married an Air OP pilot. Donald was a firm believer in charts which hung in his office and showed every imaginable graph and statistic. So when Evelyn later moved with an operational training flight to nearby Netheravon, he put up in his office there even more charts and statistics. When Donald subsequently went there to carry out a formal inspection he was somewhat surprised to find in Evelyn's office a 'Morale Chart' which showed a graph which had a line which started at the top marked 'Excellent' and had fallen to the bottom marked 'Bitched, buggered and bewildered'. Fortunately Donald had a sense of humour.

Air OP pilots learned the art of AOP flying primarily by long experience and by making their own mistakes. I could tell them all about our own experiences and mistakes and warn them of all the dangers that they might encounter. I could threaten them with court martial or the Brighton Course if they were ever to yield to the temptation to 'beat up' people or take their girl friends flying with them. But I felt that I should not lay down fixed rules as to what Air OP pilots should do and what they should not do. Our job was to support the Army ground troops in any circumstances which might arise.

There was a DH Dominie at Old Sarum and this gave me my first experience of flying with more than one engine. It was very useful when I needed to transport a number of people. It was as easy to fly as a DH82. There was also a Proctor which had, I believe, originally been a low-wing fighter trainer. It had speed and I found it very useful for flying long distances. But it had two faults. The first of these was that the perspex in front of the pilot was so worn that it was impossible to see directly in front when landing. The second of these was that when taking off along a runway with a strong cross-wind the rudder was inadequate to prevent the aircraft, when it was gathering speed, from swinging into the wind.

Pupil Air OP pilots had to take their turn to be Duty Pilots in the Watch Office. One of the duties of the Duty Pilot was to obtain 'route forecasts' of the weather, etc to any airfield to which any pilot might be about to fly. The airfields in the United Kingdom were then innumerable and some of them had most unusual names. Someone, in order to tease a new Duty Pilot, asked for a route forecast to 'Kingdom Come' and that Duty Pilot thereupon started making extensive enquiries as to where on earth 'Kingdom Come' was. And one day, when I was lecturing to a Senior Officers' Course, I was interrupted by an announcement over the Tannoy, 'Tannoy Testing, Tannoy Testing, I cannot eat my currant bun'.

On the 21st of November 1942, a Polish ATA girl, Jadwega Pilsudski (a daughter or granddaughter of the great Field Marshal and President of Poland), delivered a new aircraft to us at Old Sarum. She was an exceptionally lovely girl and I was delighted when Donald asked me to fly her to Biggin Hill to collect a fighter aircraft from there. I decided to take her in a new Vigilant which had recently been delivered to us. I made the mistake of not enquiring whether or not the compass had been 'swung', ie tested and made accurate. It had not in fact been swung and it was about 30 degrees out as far as my course to Biggin Hill was concerned.

By that time I knew all the landmarks of Southern England so well that I believed that I could never get lost anywhere. I believed that as soon as I was approaching Biggin Hill I would recognize the landmarks there. So Jadwega and I nattered away together and I never once bothered to look at the map. When the time came for us to be approaching Biggin Hill I looked around and could not see anything that I had expected to see. I was lost. This was no problem at all to anyone flying a Vigilant. I landed on a strip of grass beside a crossroads and asked someone where I was. This was a somewhat humiliating experience, but worse was to come.

After that, realizing that my compass was haywire, I followed roads to Biggin Hill. One did not approach a strange operational fighter airfield at Air OP operational height and so I climbed up to the correct height and began my approach to land. I put down full flaps and descended. Unfortunately for me the airfield 'T' was set for a landing directly downwind. This of course did not bother fighter aircraft at all as their high landing speed was such that a bit of wind behind them did not make any appreciable difference. But a Vigilant descends very slowly indeed: I have already said that it would be a sitting duck to any enemy fighter.

And so while my aircraft was waddling slowly down I saw that it was being carried by the tail-wind rather rapidly down the runway. Not wanting to risk the ultimate humiliation of over-shooting a runway suitable for fighter aircraft, I opened the throttle and went round again and then landed into wind somewhere on the grass by the Watch Office. I followed roads on the way back to Old Sarum.

At the end of the War I heard that Jadwega had been killed in a flying accident. What a tragedy.

In December 1942, Derek Heathcote-Amery, who after the War became Chancellor of the Exchequer, came to visit us at Old Sarum. He was then at the War Office and in charge of the organisation and development of the Air OP. So he decided to spend a week's leave with us and learn to fly. I got the job of teaching him and he was a delightful pupil in every way. His predecessor at the War Office had been a bit of a nuisance to us, but after Derek's visit to us he thoroughly understood all our needs and we had no further problems with the War Office. Derek later insisted on descending with the paratroops at Arnhem and I heard a report that he had been killed there. But, shortly after the War, I met him at a bus stop in Kensington and he assured me that the announcement of his death was premature. He was a very enterprising and gallant gentleman.

We were under an RAF Group in Army Co-operation Command. From time to time various very senior RAF officers came to Old Sarum, perhaps for some Senior Officers' Conference. Some of them flew themselves in and we irreverently claimed to be able to recognize their ranks by the number of 'bumps' they did on landing. By 'bump' I refer to the number of times that their aircraft hit the ground and then went up into the air again. Thus a mere Group Captain was expected to do a one-bump landing, an Air Marshal a two-bump landing and an Air Chief Marshal a three-bump landing. This of course was not really sur-prising as they had learned to fly long ago and had had very little recent practice. Air Chief Marshal 'Ugly' Barrett, AOC-in-C of Army Co-op Command, was said to 'stir the pot' during the glide before touching down. This was a practice adopted by pilots during the First World War of moving the joystick round and round in a circle in an endeavour to shorten the length of the float. There is no risk of any float or bump when one does a short landing.

In December 1942, Llewellyn flew into some HT cables and was killed. He was the first person to be killed on any Air OP Course and his death was a shock to all of us. We had liked him a lot and Donald and all us instructors went to his funeral in Wimbledon. After the funeral I went on to London and had lunch with my brother and his wife at the Mayfair. It was at that lunch that I first met Diana. It was one of those rare cases of love at first sight. We got engaged when we had only met on three occasions and we were married on the 6th of February 1943. Under such circumstances one might have expected our marriage to break up fairly soon, but in fact we have lived happily together ever since.

Our wedding in London was very much an Air OP affair. Just about all the twenty officers of 43rd OTU and a number of Bill Ballard's squadron which he was then forming at Old Sarum, came up to London for it. As I write this many years later I have before me the silver cigarette case which is inscribed with the names of the twenty officers of the OTU and we still use the mug given us by 655 AOP Squadron for putting flowers in. It was very kind of them all, particularly as at that time in the War wedding presents were almost unobtainable.

Mrs Llewellyn asked us to scatter her son's ashes from the air and this I did, one evening as the sun was setting, from a great height above Salisbury Plain. It was sweet of her to write and congratulate me on my engagement when she saw the announcement in *The Times*.

Donald was later given command of a Mosquito Squadron. The last time I saw him was when he arrived in a Mosquito to visit us at Clifton Aerodrome at York. Later he was reported missing believed killed after a Mosquito operation overseas. His body and crashed aircraft were eventually found about forty years later on a high mountain somewhere in Northern Spain. The best are always most likely to be killed in war: 'Those whom the Gods love die young.'

CHAPTER XI
Formation of 658 Air OP Squadron RAF

In April 1943, Evelyn Prendergast and I learned that we were each to form a new Air OP Squadron. His was to be 659 Squadron formed at Firbeck, and mine 658 Squadron formed at Old Sarum. Our aircraft were to be Auster IIIs which had flaps, and engines more powerful than previous Austers.

Our time with 43rd OTU enabled us to pick as our flight commanders and section officers those among our former pupils whom we particularly wanted and were still available. I chose as my flight commanders Murray Bell ('A' Flight), Tony Knight ('B' Flight) and Moke Murray ('C' Flight). I cannot speak too highly of them: there could not have been any better flight commanders, or better friends. Together we formed and trained a very efficient and happy squadron.

Forming an Air OP Squadron was by no means as easy as one might think. It was a very different unit to any known to either the Army or the RAF. Our warrant officer, flight sergeants and fitters and riggers of various RAF ranks were all 'blue jobs' and absolute experts at their own particular tasks and had never learned to do the jobs of other experts. They were used to the comforts of an RAF station.

On the other hand we had 'brown jobs'; a sergeant-major, four sergeants and a variety of other ranks who were there to do all the other jobs in the Squadron.

Out of all these specialists we had to create four teams (SHQ and the three Flights) each of which would be able to do just about any job, though the Flights could of course seek the help of the super experts of SHQ for repairing and doing major overhauls to aircraft.

For example, early in 1944, when we were under the command of the CCRA 8 Corps, Brigadier A. G. Matthew, the brigadier sent us a 3-ton truck and ordered us to convert it into a luxury caravan for his use in operations. Even he later admitted that our SHQ experts had done a superb job – at a cost to him of only fifty shillings for materials.

Every man had to learn to drive any vehicle and to be an absolute expert in map reading so that we could send him to any map reference and be certain that he would arrive there, and not get lost and blunder into the enemy front line. And our wireless operators had to make quite sure that all our wireless sets never failed us – and they never did.

In order to create such teams there had to be friendship, loyalty and indeed affection between all ranks to an extent unknown in any other unit of the three Services. When two people fly and dice with death together, a lasting bond of friendship is created.

Of course problems arose in the early days of 658 Squadron. I had learned from our unfortunate experiences of bloody-minded RAF personnel during Exercise Bumper that we must somehow get the message through to the RAF that they must only post their best men to the Air OP – men who would be willing to co-operate with us. I soon found that writing letters to Higher Authority was a waste of time, whereas much could be achieved by personal visits to the right man at the right place. The Air OP habitually operated on the 'DO' (or

Direct Officer) net. But I will say no more about this, as I think that such a net could not be used in time of peace.

At any rate we had an excellent body of 'blue jobs' posted to us. Our two blue job officers, R. McQueen (always known as 'the Adj') and Norman Foley, the Equipment Officer, between them took all the office and equipment work off my hands and I never experienced any problems with either of their departments. Norman had a special genius at ensuring that we always had rather more spare engines and mainplanes than we were entitled to. The Adj took charge of the SHQ ground column in mobile warfare and had not only to ensure that the appropriate distance was kept between vehicles, but also to map read and keep everyone off the road verges when mines were likely to be there.

The Army Depot which provided us with 'brown jobs' was not so co-operative. They believed that every Army Unit must have its fair share of 'VGVDs'. The depot was liable to collect people whom no unit wanted. I believe that every man with a 'VG' record (ie Very Good) had never been convicted of any serious military offence. A single 'dim-wit' was a menace to an Air OP squadron. One Army driver jumped out of a 15-cwt truck in Amesbury leaving it to proceed without a driver until it crashed into the bridge over the River Avon and ended up in the river. Though we were under the command of the RAF for discipline, I had to send in an accident report to Army District HQ in order to get a replacement vehicle. In the column of the accident report in which I had to state what disciplinary action had been taken against this driver, I wrote 'Sent to see a psychiatrist.' I received an indignant reply that this was not disciplinary action. As soon as the psychiatrist had arranged for this man to be posted away from my Squadron (probably to the Pioneers), I informed District HQ of this fact. I heard no more from them.

VD could be a problem. The fact that a man was being treated for venereal disease had to be kept absolutely secret. One day the Adj came to me and said that a certain gunner had applied for seven days' leave in order to get married and that the Old Sarum Medical Officer had said that this gunner was being treated for a bad case of venereal disease and would certainly communicate it to any girl with whom he had sexual intercourse. The MO had explained this to the gunner, but the gunner had replied that he knew his rights, that he was entitled to a week's leave forthwith, and that the fact of his VD must not be disclosed by anyone to anyone. So I spoke to the man, and found him adamant that he must be given leave immediately as the date of his wedding had been fixed for a few days' time. I flatly refused to grant him any leave until the MO passed him fit for marriage.

The following day a very strong-minded and indignant mother-in-law-to-be brought a bride-to-be to see me. They made a tremendous fuss and threatened to go to their Member of Parliament about my cruel and wicked behaviour. Of course I had to listen in silence and could not give any hint of my reason for refusing leave. They certainly had no knowledge of the man's VD.

I decided to seek the guidance of the very helpful Brigadier, Royal Artillery (BRA) Southern Command and he forthwith raised the matter with the GOC Southern Command, General Lloyd. I should perhaps have gone through RAF channels, but there seemed some doubt about this, and as the man was Army, I went through Army channels, and took care not to mention the man's name. The General sent me a written order that this man was not to be granted any leave at all until he had been passed fit by the MO. I much admired the General for dealing with this matter himself and for accepting full responsibility.

At the end of May 1943, I flew General Lloyd on a three-day exercise known as Exercise Columbus. I borrowed a Vigilant from 43rd OTU for this purpose as it enabled me to land him anywhere he wanted to land, including his HQ which was at the lovely Littlecote House. He was a delightful companion: generals are as a rule far more friendly than brigadiers. It was said that he was a magnificent general and that had it not been for the delicate state of his health, he would have been given the command of the 8th Army in North Africa that was given to General Montgomery. In fact General Lloyd lived to a great old age, survived General Montgomery and I heard of him not so many years ago as still alive and still Colonel of the Coldstream Guards.

I also flew on that Exercise Brigadier Staveley, BRA Southern Command, who was also a delightful passenger. He later set my Squadron our first exercise. It was very important to me that we should make a good impression and that nothing should go wrong. It was a lovely day, and I wisely chose for my SHQ ALG the delightful village of Crawley (one of the most beautiful villages in England), and my Flight ALGs were chosen in the valley of the River Test. Amid such surroundings the Brigadier obviously enjoyed that exercise.

By the time that we went to Normandy, I think I had somehow or other weeded out all the soldiers who should never have been posted to an Air OP Squadron.

My Squadron was officially under the command of the AOC of a Fighter Group whose HQ was at Bath. To my surprise and pleasure the AOC, Air Marshal Sir Charles Steele, KCB, DFC, invited me to lunch with him, sat me next to him and treated me with great courtesy and friendliness. I suppose he was treating me in the same way as he treated all fighter squadron commanders newly placed under his command, but I was immensely impressed. After the Battle of Britain all fighter pilots were regarded as heroes.

Shortly after 658 Squadron was formed, I received an order to deliver an aircraft, which was surplus to our establishment, to Speke (which is now the Liverpool Airport). This involved my sending two pilots in two aircraft to Speke and both pilots were then to return to Old Sarum in one aircraft. I sent Sandeman and Bogod. They were both killed when their aircraft hit a tree on the return journey and crashed beside the River Avon near Larkhill. This was a bad start for my Squadron. The RAF were most kind and understanding and did not enquire too closely into the delicate question as to precisely why they had hit that tree.

After this disaster I thought a great deal about what I could do to prevent such a thing ever happening again. It seemed to me that when a young and inexperienced pilot is flying alone he will take care of himself. But the competitive spirit between young men is such that when two of them are flying together, whether in one or two aircraft, one or both of them may take risks which are quite unreasonable and daredevil. It is a case of 'whatever you can do, I can do better'. When I had been flying as a passenger of Evelyn, he had on occasion given me a bit of anxiety neurosis by doing very steep turns round haystacks, though I naturally concealed any alarm that I might have felt. I decided that no threats of court martial or the Brighton Course would be likely to deter young men from behaving like young men. The only possible remedy was to explain the risks and to ask them to do their utmost to resist temptation. And I frowned on the practising of evasive tactics. Apart from Alan Gee, whose death was in no way his own fault, no other pilot of my Squadron was killed or seriously injured during the War in any flying accident.

Alan Gee was killed when he was with Moke Murray's 'C' Flight then stationed at Doncaster: my Squadron HQ were at Burn which was a Lancaster Operational Bomber Station. Alan was seen to be flying quite normally when suddenly his aircraft went into a spiral dive into the ground. In fact I think it was upside-down when it hit the ground. As we had just been equipped with the new Auster IV, I immediately suspected structural failure and requested an investigation by the AID (Accident Investigation Department). The

Auster IV had had some problem before and we did not want pilots to suspect the airworthiness of their new aircraft.

The AID were at first inclined to the view that Alan must have been doing unauthorised aerobatics and that this had caused the crash. But they changed their minds when I told them of my own experience when flying with Monty from Burn at the same hour as when Alan was killed. There was a strong wind that day with some terrible gusts. Each gust hit the aircraft like a hammer blow and I soon decided that, unless I returned to Burn as quickly as possible and landed there, the aircraft would soon break up. Alan's death proved to us that one should never fly a slow light aircraft in such conditions of gustiness. But that was the only time that I ever encountered such hammer blows. We later heard reports that an Auster of another squadron had broken up in similar weather conditions in the mountains of Wales.

I learnt, when visiting 'A' Flight when they were taking part in an Army exercise in the hills of Angus, that on a very windy day one must keep above the tops of the hills and must not go down and land in fields in the glens. The reason is fairly obvious. Just imagine an Auster flying along a glen in complete shelter from the wind and then it rounds a corner and is suddenly struck by a westerly near gale force wind. And the wind in glens is constantly coming from different directions. Diana and I have a guest house, which was an ancient farmhouse, near the top of a hill close to our home. When there is a strong wind it blows round and round the house and there is no shelter anywhere. Austers were not built to stand such strains. Incidentally our Austers cost under £1,000 in 1943. Nowadays, forty years later, modern aircraft may cost millions and travel at very high speeds and they would probably scarcely notice such gusts.

CHAPTER XII
Evasive Tactics

There is a note on page 161 of *Unarmed into Battle* which reads, 'The relatively high proportion of casualties due to flying accidents, both at home and in theatres of war, is mainly accounted for by the hazards of low flying.' I personally would have substituted for the words 'low flying' the words 'practising evasive tactics'. After Bill Ballard and Benson had been killed in April 1943, when practising evasive tactics, I resolved that such practice should never be carried out by any of my Squadron. And we never had a single aircraft shot down by enemy fighters during the War, though very few of our pilots did not experience at least one of such attacks. It is pointless to teach young men to fly dangerously: this comes quite naturally to them. Evasive tactics involve ignoring all the rules for correct flying and concentrating on one thing only – preventing the enemy aircraft pointing its guns at you.

The Lysander aircraft flown by Army Co-operation pilots before the fall of France in May 1940 had suffered appalling casualties as a result of being shot down by enemy fighters. Few of these pilots had survived, but one who did survive was S/Ldr Peter Hurndall, DFC who, after being wounded by a bullet through his head, escaped an enemy fighter by some brilliant low flying. As a result of his wound Peter was later given a non-flying job at Old Sarum. He and I used to do some interesting low flying together in a Vigilant across the country of the Blackmore Vale. Naturally we discussed the problems of evasive tactics.

The Lysander was too large and not sufficiently manoeuvrable. It had some armament but not enough for defence against enemy fighters. It could land and take off out of large fields but not small ones. It was quite useless for anything other than landing people by night in occupied France or fetching them home again.

The experiences of Lysander pilots in France in May 1940, led the Air Officer Commander-in-Chief, Army Co-operation Command, to state (I quote from *Unarmed into Battle*) that in his considered opinion the Air OP would be unable to operate in the face of the enemy, that it would be 'entirely vulnerable to any enemy fighter which cared to shoot it down', and that it could not operate from enclosed country.

In the very early days of the Air OP, a famous fighter pilot was invited to come to Larkhill and give us a lecture on evasive tactics. He was not very encouraging. He indicated that he had little doubt that he could shoot down a whole squadron of our Taylorcraft within a few minutes. 'Why,' he said, 'I could bugger you with my slipstream.' His mistake was that he imagined that Air OP pilots would stay high up in the air and try to escape enemy aircraft by outflying them. We didn't. As soon as we saw an enemy fighter we either got into the nearest cloud or got down to just above ground level. It would be suicide for an enemy fighter to chase an Auster round trees just behind our front line: the entire British Army would be firing at the fighter.

In those early days we occasionally got Spitfires or Hurricanes to come and play at evasive tactics with us. This was not particularly dangerous provided we did the sensible thing and let them win. There was no point in our trying to be too clever and for example, flying under HT cables in the hope that the fighter would hit the cables! But to send up two of our pilots in Austers to do mock battle really was dangerous. Pilots would do hair-raising things merely for the satisfaction of being able to say that they had 'won'.

Many Air OP pilots had a great deal more experience of enemy fighters than I ever did. Several of them were shot down and I know a few of these who lived to fly again. But far more Air OP pilots were killed practising evasive tactics in England than were ever killed by enemy fighters in all theatres of war. As I have already said, it is absurd to teach young men to fly dangerously: this comes quite naturally to them.

In Normandy I had a few fleeting experiences with enemy fighters, but it was never more than one pass after which the fighter went on with its more important business. And there was one occasion when Sam Maidment (who had been my driver/batman since the beginning of the War) was driving me near the runway of an RAF aerodrome at the very moment when an Me109 was coming very low down that runway in the hope of catching some of our aircraft on it. There were no such aircraft and so he swerved slightly and opened fire with his machine-guns on my staff car. He was obviously unaware of my own unimportance. Sam put his foot hard down on the brake and the car stopped abruptly. We saw the bullets flash by about a foot in front of the windscreen. The aircraft was so low that any RAF guns which might have been there were unable to fire at all.

There were a number of occasions when the sound of a succession of Bren guns firing signalled the approach of a very low flying enemy fighter whose pilot had decided that it might be safer for him to fly very low on his mission rather than to risk our fighters and anti-aircraft guns which would have dealt with him if he had been higher up. But our light anti-aircraft fire nearly always got him sooner or later. As I write this I am thinking of an Me109 which passed over our ALG at St Gabriel only a few feet up. He was then obviously wounded or killed as his aircraft suddenly went into a steep climb and then received a direct hit from an anti-aircraft gun and became a ball of flame. I was surprised to experience a feeling of regret at the death of a brave young man – even though he was an enemy.

Unfortunately the training in aircraft recognition of many of our soldiers was clearly inadequate and they frequently mistook one of our Mustangs for an Me109. Once someone had started firing at one of our own aircraft, others did likewise. On such occasions I would send someone in a jeep to deliver the necessary rockets to nearby units who had blundered in this manner. Eventually, on the 17th of July 1944, in order to stop this occurring, the Army Commander issued an order forbidding firing at any aircraft more than 5,000 yards behind the front line. Thereafter the protection Air OP aircraft received from our fire from the ground was diminished.

On the 3rd of February 1945, the Army Commander, General Sir Miles Dempsey, sent for me and asked me to do a photo run for him of the River Maas the whole length of the Army front down to Venlo in the South. He told me that the purpose of this photo run was to assist in a decision as to where the river was to be crossed and the photographs should therefore, show clearly all possible forming up places on our side of the river and also a considerable area on the far side. I decided that the photographs would have to be considerably more vertical than those which I usually took and that for this purpose it would be necessary for me to fly at 4,000 feet. On this occasion I did not take an observer up with me. This may have been a mistake, but the Auster was far more manoeuvrable without a passenger. We were equipped with chest parachutes but we rarely used them: I did not believe it to be possible to 'bale out' of an Auster and I never heard of anyone succeeding in doing this. If a pilot did take an observer up with him a parachute would obviously have been useless : no pilot could bale out and leave his observer to die.

I climbed up to 4,000 feet, got into position, started the camera and began the run. It was a beautiful day and perfect in every way for photography. I had to keep on an absolutely even keel and to watch the camera sights continuously. The front seemed very quiet and no enemy anti-aircraft guns fired at me. I was enjoying myself as I always did during photo runs when there were no 'unfriendly noises' to disturb my concentration.

However, it so happened that two enemy Focke-Wolfe 190 fighters came across the river, shot down and killed Stuart of 659 Squadron and then turned their attention on me. I did not see Stuart being shot down and I only became aware of the presence of the enemy fighters when the entire British Army suddenly seemed to be firing at me. I quickly looked round and saw one FW190 coming at me from slightly above and the other from below. They would have found it much easier to shoot me down if they had come at me from behind. The British Army were shooting at them and any bursts near me were unintended.

On such occasions one does not think of evasive tactics. And strangely enough one is far too busy to be alarmed. The adrenalin flows and one has a sense of exhilaration. I remember my neck going round and round as if made of rubber. And I remember getting out of the sights of one FW190 by diving and at the same time applying full rudder, and in the course of dodging the other I went into an almost vertical spiral dive during which I noticed that my airspeed was in excess of the speed at which the wings were expected to come off. Then I had to pull up steeply again because the first enemy fighter had somehow got below me and was coming at me from another direction. This was annoying because my intended destination was down below the tree tops where the British Army might succeed in hitting my pursuers.

After what seemed an age, two Spitfire XIIs (which were special new Spitfires with a very distinctive appearance) arrived on the scene and as a nice little gesture which I much appreciated, passed one on each side of me and then chased the enemy fighters across the River Maas. Enemy fighters did not bother Austers when there were British fighters about.

I did not wait to see what happened next. I got down to tree top level, flew north to the spot where I had started that photo run, climbed back up to 4,000 feet, and started the run again.

One cannot offer an Army Commander a set of photographs which is not continuous. That second run was uneventful, and the photographs were perhaps the best that I ever took. One photograph of the destroyed bridge at Venlo was subsequently enlarged by the Kinema Branch of Second Army and as I am writing this now I have before me a letter from them saying, 'I think it will interest you to know that the photo taken by your Squadron of Venlo Bridge has been of the greatest value both to the British 2nd Army and the Ninth US Army.' I believe some gallant American soldiers managed to cross this bridge despite the fact that the Germans had blown it up. I think the thanks were really due to those two Spitfire pilots.

When I was awarded the French Croix de Guerre, the BRA told me that it was the Army Commander who had insisted that one of those which he had at his disposal should go to me. He had naturally heard of my little adventure which the Army had watched with interest.

CHAPTER XIII
Night Flying

Early dawn and late dusk were the two best times for us to spot the flashes of enemy artillery firing. Anyone, who has ridden a horse home at dusk after a day's hunting, knows that there comes a time when the sparks created by the horse's shoes on the road become clearly visible. And as it gets darker and darker one's eyes become increasingly able to see in the dark. The eyes of youth seem particularly to have this ability. I believe bomber pilots wore dark glasses for a considerable time before they took off on a night bombing raid.

In the winter of 1944/5 generals who flew as passengers in Austers to attend important conferences were not easily persuaded by their pilots that they must hurry home before dark. And we did not want the locations of our ALGs not far behind the front line to be disclosed to the enemy by the firing of Very lights. In fact our only flarepath consisted of two green hurricane lamps. I was habitually alarmed in Normandy by Oliver Murphy's habit of landing the Army Commander at his Tac ALG in the early dark and then flying home in the black dark to our SHQ ALG. But he always arrived safely.

In the early days of 658 Squadron when we were at Old Sarum, I gave every pilot a considerable amount of instruction in night flying. We started with dusk circuits and then went on to do circuits in the black dark. I particularly enjoyed this on a summer evening. Each circuit took us over Salisbury and there we could see every infringement of the black-out regulations.

In due course I thought the pilots were ready to do their first dusk cross-country flight. The events of 'B' Flight's first dusk cross-country flight I described in an obituary which I wrote of Claud Cecil Ballyn, DFC and Bar. I intend to include that obituary at the end of these Memoirs and so I will not relate here the events of that evening. The nervous strain on me of it convinced me that any further experiments in night flying must be carried out by myself alone.

Monty, our wireless expert, designed a method of sending out a beam (such as that used by bombers) using a long piece of wire, a windscreen wiper and an Army wireless set. If one was on the beam one heard a continuous note: one side of the beam one heard a series of dots, and the other side a series of dashes. It worked perfectly.

At the beginning of May 1944, I did several 'beam approach tests' by day. The next thing we wanted was a quieter aircraft which the enemy would be unlikely to hear when we were flying at night. The Auster manufacturers at Rearsby were always willing to help us in any way they could and, on the 1st of May, Mr A. L. Wykes flew down to us a prototype Auster fitted with a silencer. The silencer was excellent but the loss of power due to it was unacceptable.

On the 10th of May, I did a night cross-country flight lasting an hour which was timed to end at first light by which time the beam should have taken me over Gatwick, which was then an RAF grass field. Monty was in charge of the beam. It was a most peaceful and enjoyable night flight until the beginning of first light when I flew into an early morning mist. The beam took me directly over Gatwick and fortunately I spotted an aircraft on the ground below me there. I landed more or less blind but safely and I had difficulty in finding my way to the Watch Office in the mist. I decided not to do any more night cross-country flights unless they were absolutely necessary.

CHAPTER XIV
Discipline

The activities of an Air OP Squadron were so varied that it was very difficult for even its squadron commander to say precisely what was permissible and what was not permissible. Every pilot was expected to become an expert at not only conducting live shoots but also at each of the following things: landing and taking off out of every possible variety of small field and in every condition of wind and ground surface; dropping a message bag with such accuracy that it invariably fell at the feet of the intended recipient; doing low flying cross-country flights and never getting lost; learning from long experience what foul weather an Air OP pilot could possibly fly through in order to meet his obligations to the Army and at maintaining the morale of all those under him by ensuring that they were at all times well fed and never more uncomfortable than was absolutely necessary.

Some squadron commanders would have added to the above list evasive tactics and the firing of recognition signals from Austers. But, as I have said, I disapproved of evasive tactics and was not very keen on the firing of Very pistols from aircraft after a pilot of another squadron had shot himself down in flames by doing this.

We were of course aware of both the Army and the RAF orders and regulations but many of these should not, in our view, have been applied to an Air OP Squadron. For example, only a Fitter E (Engines) was allowed by the RAF to swing a prop, and no prop was to be swung unless proper chocks were in front of the wheels. Every flight had to be properly authorised and to be solely for training purposes and not for the convenience or pleasure of the pilot. But what if the training purposes happened to coincide with the convenience and pleasure of the pilot? It was very difficult to draw the line and so, when drawing it, we naturally allowed ourselves to be influenced by the morale of the Squadron.

For instance there was the 'egg round'. On exercises it was surely justifiable for a pilot to be instructed to land in fields beside farmhouses and there purchase eggs or butter. And if we had carried in our aircraft the extremely heavy RAF chocks, we could not have used the small fields which we frequently did use.

Then there was the problem of girl friends or girls who might become friends. An instructor or a squadron or flight commander would give a pilot a map reference and tell him to do a low flying cross-country flight to that map reference, select an ALG there and land in it and then fly home again. Why should not the instructing pilot give the other pilot a map reference which happened to be the home of friends of the former. I remember 'Curly' Wood (who in fact was bald) expressing some surprise when he landed me at Sutton Bingham Manor near Yeovil and an attractive girl came up to us and had a chat. It is surely better to land where one is going to be welcomed, than meet an indignant farmer. Having lived in Dorset and Somerset. I could call on so many people I wanted to see and at the same time give instruction to pupils.

On one occasion I organized a squadron exercise in which my three Flights were each to find themselves ALGs in the neighbourhood of Sherborne Park and then send a pilot with each of the three ALG map references to be dropped by message bag beside my staff car wherever that might be. I was outside Sherborne Abbey with my staff car when three aircraft flew over low and dropped message bags at my feet. The Flights were then moved to the area of Cadbury Castle and the next lot of message bags were dropped beside me when I was in my aunt's garden at Queen Camel.

Was there anything wrong in this? I certainly did not think so at the time. The people of Sherborne and of Queen Camel appeared to be delighted by the entertainment: certainly no one made any complaint. But when I had been in Tetley's Flight of 651 Squadron at Winchester early in February 1942, people certainly complained to Worthy Down Naval Air Station of our low flying and they passed the complaints on to us – they never reached Higher Authority and in any event no one knew what we were entitled to do. Even we were not sure of the answer to this. We were using a rather inadequate field on the hill above Winchester Castle.

As I am a historian, this field was of some interest to me. Waltheof was the last Anglo-Saxon Earl and he was sentenced to death quite unjustly for treason against William the Conqueror. As the Normans feared that the Anglo-Saxons in Winchester might try to stop the execution, he was taken at dawn to the field which we were using as an ALG and told to put his head on a block there. But he asked to be allowed to say his prayers before the headsman struck. These prayers became interminable and a crowd of Anglo-Saxons was beginning to gather there. He had just said '. . . and lead us not into temptation' when the headsman struck and severed his head with one blow: whereupon the severed head uttered, 'but deliver us from evil.' This 'miracle' led the Anglo-Saxons to revere him as a saint; for many years to come they made pilgrmages to his shrine and miraculous cures were reported.

In the early days of 651 Squadron, Evelyn Prendergast had a girl friend who was a VAD at the Army hospital near Shaftesbury. One day when we were on an exercise he was ordered to leave immediately for Northern Ireland where he was to carry out a lecture tour on the Air OP. There was only one way in which Evelyn could inform his girl friend that he would be unable to keep their date for that evening: he took it. He wrote a note, 'Sorry darling, unable to see you tonight', addressed it to her, put it in a message bag, and flew over to the hospital and dropped the message bag near some people who were standing outside.

Unfortunately a general was in the act of carrying out a formal inspection of the hospital, and, seeing the message land, demanded that it should be brought to him. He then insisted on the VAD disclosing the name of the writer of the note. Charles Bazeley later sent for Evelyn, gave him a rocket and told him that RAF Higher Authority were insisting that he be court-martialled for a flying offence. After a pause Charles added that on the day of Evelyn's offence he was still subject to Army discipline and that it was only on the following day that all Air OP officers became subject to RAF discipline. Army discipline was not concerned with flying offences and therefore Evelyn would hear no more about this matter.

I personally cannot see what Evelyn did wrong. It was not his fault that he was unable to keep that evening's date. No one would have objected if he had delivered the message in a jeep. A jeep journey would have taught him nothing, whereas a journey by aircraft gave him some practice in message dropping.

The daughters who had lived in the country houses of Britain before the War had mostly disappeared into the various women's services. But they still went home on leave from time to time and there were many attractive 'land girls'. When we were in Yorkshire there was attached to my Squadron a supernumerary pilot (we called him 'Prune') who habitually got lost when I sent him to practise short landings in fields. He would return hours later and fail to give any adequate explanation. I suspected a girl friend. I met him many years later, when he was being fitted for a pair of Purdey guns at the West London Shooting School, and I asked him about this. He replied that he and that girl friend had just celebrated their silver wedding.

Perhaps I should explain what the name 'Prune' meant in those days. RAF manuals contained comic sketches of a mythical pilot officer – Prune – who invariably did everything wrong. This was an excellent way of teaching pilots by getting them to learn from Prune's mistakes. Prune was said to have 'destroyed seventeen aircraft, all of them our own!'

When we were at Hartfield a certain gunner urgently needed forty-eight hours compassionate leave to go home to Canterbury. I flew him there and landed him beside the river near the Cathedral. I saw nothing wrong in this, but I would probably have been in trouble if I had damaged the aircraft in landing.

I heard after the War that about two months before we went to Normandy, when I was on a week's leave, an aircraft of my Squadron had landed in a park on the outskirts of London, that a passenger with a suitcase had got out, that the aircraft had then taken off again, and that a police officer had then chased the passenger but had failed to catch him. Unfortunately someone had taken the aircraft's number.

Ian McNaughton, the Squadron Captain, somehow persuaded the Adj to agree that I would not be told of this. Between them, and without my knowledge, they carried on evasive correspondence tactics with the Air Ministry until we went to Normandy. Thereafter the Air Ministry no longer bothered us. It would have been silly of them to have done so as the offender might have been killed.

On our ALGs the ground crews were available to swing our props, but when we were alone in a field somewhere we had to swing our own props. Some Auster aircraft refused to start unless the throttle was opened quite a bit. As I have said, the correct drill was to put chocks in front of the wheels to prevent the aircraft moving off as soon as the engine fired. But chocks were unacceptable additional weight in the aircraft, hence our habit of putting our tin hat in front of one wheel and our gas mask in front of the other. As soon as the engine fired we throttled back, removed the tin hat and gas mask and then climbed into the aircraft.

But if the throttle had to be opened a lot in order to encourage the engine to start, when it eventually did so it sometimes caused the aircraft to push the gas mask aside and then swing round until it was free of the tin hat also. The pilot would then have to get out of the way of the prop and scramble into a moving aircraft. I have heard many stories of accidents caused by aircraft moving off faster than the pilot could run.

One of my flight commanders, Murray Bell, had such an experience. He was alone and swinging his own prop during an exercise. As the engine would not start, he decided to follow the drill when the mixture had become too rich. This was to switch off, open the throttle fully and then swing the prop in order to 'blow out'. Unfortunately he forgot to switch off. The engine started with a roar and the aircraft shook itself free of his gas mask and tin hat, and moved off at speed. But for some reason it went round in circles and behaved as if it was deliberately chasing its would-be occupant. Instead of Murray running after it, he had to run to get out of the way. Fortunately, we managed to repair that aircraft ourselves and thereby avoided an accident report, which would have led to trouble with the Air Ministry.

I had one disastrous experience of this problem. On the 19th of November 1943, when my Squadron was at York, I was summoned to Corps Headquarters at Sand Hutton. I usually flew there and landed in an adjoining field. As I was taking an aircraft that was extremely difficult to start, I hurriedly asked Mr Easton, the Warrant Officer, to spare me a fitter who would go with me in order to swing the prop for the return journey. Unfortunately he sent with me AC Brotherton, a rigger (airframe fitter) who had only been posted to us a few days before and who had never swung a prop.

When the time came for Brotherton to swing the prop, it immediately became obvious that he was frightened of it and that it would certainly never start for him. So I placed him in the pilot's seat, opened the throttle quite a bit, and showed him how to close it as soon as the engine fired. Then I swung the prop myself. The engine started at the first swing and Brotherton immediately opened to full throttle. My shouts to him were drowned by the roar of the engine as the aircraft began to move off, while he hugged the stick and otherwise did precisely nothing. I hung on to the end of a wing strut and kept shouting to him to throttle back or switch off. The aircraft went round and round in ever-widening circles and finally flung me off and rushed at a hedge. I feared that it might take off and that I would be responsible for that airman's death. However, as it crashed into the hedge, he at last switched off.

As the aircraft was seriously damaged, I had to send in an accident report: as I had been the pilot it was my accident even though I was not in the aircraft at the time. Group was as usual kind and understanding and I only received a mild rocket. During the France/Germany Campaign we frequently flew generals about the battle front and landed them in fields where there were no ground crews. It became an Air OP joke that every pilot had to learn the correct method of saluting a general who was taking off without him.

CHAPTER XV

With 8 Corps

We moved from Old Sarum to Oatlands Hill to make room at Old Sarum for another squadron. On the 28th of August 1943, I took the Squadron on a route march to Stonehenge: it was good exercise as well as interesting for everyone. There was a civilian attendant there who expressed the opinion that even the Army and RAF ought to pay an entrance fee and that climbing over the surrounding wire fence was not the correct manner of entering, but our majority view prevailed. On our return journey to Oatlands Hill, Ian MacNaughton, who had been left behind to hold the fort, arrived on a motorcycle with a written order that we were all to move forthwith to York where we were to be under the command of the CCRA 8 Corps. We arrived at York the following day. Our happy days with Southern Command were over.

The CCRA 8 Corps was Brigadier A. G. Matthew, nicknamed 'Hammer'. He was a martinet and I did not much care for his habit of sending me orders which began, 'You will state without delay why . . .' He had a reputation for breaking officers whom he did not like very quickly indeed. It was said that a new Intelligence Officer had recently been posted under his command and at their first meeting, Hammer had asked the Intelligence Officer, 'What is the altitude of the Pole Star?' The latter replied that he did not know and was forthwith sacked for his lack of intelligence. I always felt that Hammer did not particularly like me but though I was temporarily under his command, my Squadron was destined to be the 2nd Army Squadron and sacking me would have required the agreement of the BRA, Jack Parham.

My Squadron were to share Clifton Aerodrome, York, with Evelyn's 659 Squadron and Evelyn and I had always been and have always remained, close friends. It was a great pleasure to me to be with him again. From the very start we had problems with the RAF Camp Commandant of Clifton who was quite unable to accept that there was any difference between Air OP Squadrons and RAF Squadrons. He was constantly requiring us to provide more men to do fatigues on the aerodrome than we felt that we could spare and there were many other trivial things about which he complained. We were certain that we needed all our chaps to go with us on every exercise. However, that Camp Commandant was later replaced by Heaton-Armstrong, the Chester Herald, and we both got on splendidly with him.

Not long after our arrival in York, I received an order to take all my officers to meet the BRA. I left the Adj and Norman Foley, our two RAF officers, to hold the fort at Clifton. The BRA, who after the War became Major-General Jack Parham and one of the two joint authors of *Unarmed into Battle*, was friendly and delightful in every way. We returned to Clifton in time for lunch and there I was told by the Adj that in my absence an order had come from CCRA 8 Corps instructing me to send a pilot with aircraft immediately to 8 Corps HQ at Sand Hutton to fly a Brigadier Lewis from there to London. Unfortunately the Adj had replied that the RAF Communications Flight which had recently been at Clifton was no longer there and that an Air OP Squadron did not provide communications flights. This information was certainly the orthodox Air OP view, but had become somewhat old-fashioned. Hammer regarded this as a refusal to obey a direct order. A few minutes later Major Grec, Hammer's GII, telephoned me and said 'You will state without delay in writing why, etc ...' I wisely replied that we would of course send an aircraft to Sand Hutton immediately. We were just in time to intercept Brigadier Lewis when he was about to catch a train to London and Jimmy Storie then flew him to an airfield near London. I gave Jimmy permission to spend that night in London and told him to fly back to us at York the following day. I was not particularly keen on sending pilots on such long communication flights as, if we had killed a brigadier, there would have been hell to pay. Later I became accustomed to having to accept this risk.

My next spot of bother with Hammer was when I had received an imperative order from the Air Ministry, which was sent to all Air OP squadron commanders, that in future no Air OP pilot was ever to land in any field which he had not first walked on the ground. This was an order which could not possibly be obeyed if the Air OP were to continue to be of any use to the Army. I drafted a reply very carefully, pointing out to the Air Ministry what this order would mean. My mistake was to send, out of courtesy, copies of the Air Ministry's letter and my reply thereto to RA 8 Corps.

Hammer sent for me: his face was scarlet with rage. He did all the talking while I remained absolutely silent. I had committed the appalling and unpardonable crime of arguing about an order which I had received. Orders must be obeyed without question or argument. When he finally ceased speaking, I attempted to say something about the absurdity of that particular order. The gist of his reply was that when an officer received an absurd order he must just say 'Yes, Sir,' though he may subsequently find it impossible to obey.

I with some difficulty refrained from saying that, though this might be the correct drill in the Army, it would be very dangerous in the RAF. When a pilot next crashed in a field which he had not already visited, the RAF might then require him to be court-martialled for having disobeyed this order. I would then as squadron commander have had to intervene by saying that I had not passed this order on to my pilots, or that I had told them to ignore it because it was so absurd. I would then have been court-martialled. It is surely far better to anticipate trouble and take prompt evasive action than to obey the book of rules and blunder into a disaster.

Now I am going to digress and describe an incident which occurred a few days after all hostilities in Germany had ceased. The Army Commander told me that he was going to need quite a number of pilots and aircraft for flying generals to various Russian Army Head-quarters and elsewhere. I said that I would need to fetch my 'B' Flight from Kiel to help in this. I had just visited Tony Knight's Flight who were then under Hammer's command at Kiel Aerodrome and I knew that they wanted to join us at Lüneberg. So an order was immediately sent by the Army Commander through RA 8 Corps recalling 'B' Flight to my Squadron Headquarters ALG at Lüneberg. Shortly afterwards a very worried Tony arrived by air from Kiel and told me that Hammer had told him that he was quite unable to allow him to go for another two or three weeks! I got through on the telephone to Dickie Dawson, an ADC, and told him what had happened. A few minutes later Dickie rang back and said that if my 'B' Flight had not arrived at my ALG by 0800 hrs the following morning the Army Commander was to be informed immediately. In fact 'B' Flight arrived with time to spare. Even a brigadier must not argue about orders.

The winter of 1943/4 was for us a period of intensive training: shoots on all the Artillery

Ranges in the North of England, Flight Exercises, Squadron Exercises, Corps Exercises and Army Exercises. There were trials of the waterproofing of all Army vehicles in preparation for a landing on some beach somewhere on the Continent. For this purpose something resembling a lengthy swimming pool with ramps down into it at each end was constructed. January was not a good time to enter a swimming pool, even with all one's clothing on. I remember watching a jeep do a trial at this. For a few seconds the jeep floated: then it sank to the bottom and its wheels propelled it through the water while the driver, with only his head above the water, clung desperately to the steering wheel. A special pipe carried the exhaust to well above the driver's head.

On one Corps or Army Exercise my Squadron Headquarters moved all their aircraft and vehicles into a field in Yorkshire. No question of trespass arose in time of war. As a matter of courtesy I sent 'Prune' Harding to see the farmer and obtain his permission and co-operation. Prune returned and told us that the farmer was very angry indeed and had given us ten minutes to get all our aircraft and vehicles off his land and had indicated that he intended to complain to Higher Authority if we failed to comply with this demand.

So I sent Monty to see the farmer, and he soon returned with permission to stay where we were for as long as we liked, permission to buy as many eggs and as much butter and milk as we wanted and an invitation to the officers to sleep on the floor of the farmhouse sitting-room and to all other ranks to sleep under cover of various farm buildings. That evening we had a most enjoyable game of dominoes with the farmer and his wife.

Monty was invaluable to me because of his genius for obtaining permission for all sorts of things. One day he and I were at Hatfield Aerodrome visiting one of my Flights which was then there. He knew that one of my ambitions was to fly a Mosquito and he persuaded John De Havilland to take me up on one of his test flights. John was one of the great sons of the great De Havilland family who between them probably did more to win the War than any other family. John did the usual aerobatics and other tests which culminated in a power dive at an immense speed and pulling out of the dive so abruptly that my head and shoulders felt as if they were being driven through the seat on which I was sitting. So much blood ran from my head that I experienced difficulty in seeing at all. It was my first experience of massive 'G'. Then John invited me to fly the aircraft and I found it a joy to fly. But I was glad that John himself landed it as only a genius could land a Mosquito at its very high landing speed on that comparatively small grass aerodrome. Alas, John was killed in a flying collision there only about a fortnight later.

At York we became friendly with the pilots of the nearby bomber squadron at Rufforth. We naturally wanted to fly their bombers and they, our Austers. We of course each flew the other's aircraft as second pilots: the first pilot has to take the blame for any accident. I see in my log book that on the 11th of November 1943, I flew a Halifax as second pilot and the 'Duty' was described as 'Evasive Tactics'.

Occasionally Hammer set my Squadron or one of my Flights an exercise which he person-ally watched. It was most important to me that everything should go like clockwork. I had learned from Roscoe Turner in the Dorset Yeomanry the maxim that when the battery commander comes on parade everyone must be ready to move off. It was not a job of the battery or squadron commander to run round in circles chasing people so as to have them ready in time. I did eventually succeed in getting my officers to have everyone ready in time. Incidentally I never succeeded in getting my wife and children to comply with this rule.

One evening I received a message from Hammer ordering me to have my 'B' Flight at a given map reference by 0900 hrs the following morning and stating that he, the CCRA, would attend the Flight's exercise. My other two Flights were then away doing live shoots on artillery ranges.

The following morning, at the prescribed hour, I had everything absolutely ready in the field at the map reference which I had been given. I sent Tony Knight, the Flight Commander, up to give me early warning over the wireless of the CCRA's approach. When Hammer arrived in his staff car he announced his intention to inspect the Flight. In this context 'inspection' means asking everyone difficult questions in the expectation of finding something to criticize.

Then a wireless operator came running up to me with a message which had just been received. Hammer said to the man 'Give me the message' and took it from him. He read the message, frowned, handed it to Major Grec, his GII, and said, 'What does this mean?' Grec replied, 'It is obviously in code' and, plainly trying hard not to laugh, passed the message on to me. The message read, 'Carpenter's tool now arriving at ALG'. What was I to do? A mere major does not call an inspecting brigadier by his nickname and certainly does not encode that as a 'carpenter's tool'. I knew that if I didn't do something quickly, Hammer was going to ask me to decode that message.

So I shouted to everyone on the field. 'The ALG is being shelled! Move to alternative ALG.' Immediately there was intense activity everywhere, pilots ran to their aircraft and took off, the vehicles were started up and driven off and in a minute or two the field was empty apart from the CCRA, Grec and I and our staff cars and drivers. I think it was Charles Ballyn who did most to take the Brigadier's mind off carpenter's tools. After taking off he kept his aircraft only two or three feet above the ground and for a few seconds it looked, both to the CCRA and to me, that he was going to crash into the line of trees at the end of the field. At the very last moment he pulled steeply up over the trees and then dived down again out of our sight. This led to a conversation with Hammer as to the training of our pilots in the difficult art of never disclosing to the enemy the locations of ALGs. The rest of that exercise went without a hitch and the subject of carpenters' tools was not mentioned again.

In the spring of 1944, my three Flights were each from time to time attached to divisions with which they might be working after we had gone overseas. They were trained by then and had to learn to be fairly independent of my SHQ. One day I visited 'A' Flight which was then at Penshurst. Jimmy Storie was in that Flight and he had been an artist before the War.

Their Officers' Mess at Penshurst was in a fairly large unfurnished house. I found a large room there one wall of which had been decorated completely by a most artistic mural which depicted a scene off the southern coast of England, a girl standing naked up to her knees in the sea, an Auster flying above her and its pilot leaning out of it and staring at the girl. I wonder what the owner of that house subsequently thought of that picture. The last I heard of Jimmy was that he was a lecturer in art at Edinburgh University.

On the 16th of December 1943, we were sent to South Wales to do some flights across the Bristol Channel to the coast of Devon. This was to prepare us for a flight overseas to wherever we might be going to land on the Continent of Europe. The first of these flights was from St Athan to Westonzoyland which was close to the site of the Battle of Sedgemoor which took place in 1685. There we had to find a field and then return to St Athan. At RAF Station St Athan there was a swimming pool in which we were invited to practise climbing into RAF rubber dinghies, with which we would be equipped for our flights overseas. I do not think any Air OP pilot ever had to use a dinghy, but after the War mine came in very useful as a paddling pool for the children.

The second of these flights was from St Govan's Head, near Tenby, to Cleave, near Bude:

this was a most interesting flight as our course took us directly over Lundy Island. We each flew alone and separately, so as to give us some experience of the loneliness which a pilot feels when he is flying alone and out of sight of any land. I noticed that, because of this feeling of loneliness, one or two of the pilots persisted in talking over the wireless throughout the journey. I had only permitted them to be in touch by wireless with a ground station just in case anyone should have an engine failure. I told them that there would be wireless silence during their flights to the Continent.

I warned them to keep above 50 feet when travelling over the sea. Judging height when flying over the sea is very deceptive and it is dangerous to play games with the tops of waves as, if an aircraft's wheels so much as touch a wave, it tips forward and goes into 'the drink'. During the War 'going into the drink' meant 'ditching' it in the sea.

We spent Christmas at RAF Station Manorbier where the station commander's job was to play with unmanned light aircraft controlled by radio from the ground. I say 'play' because it must have been enormous fun.

Diana was able to spend a few days with me over Christmas at Tenby: she was then three months pregnant and had as a result obtained her release from the WRENs. Those were very happy days: Hammer was far away in Yorkshire.

In the early months of 1944, we were 'mobilised'. Mobilisation meant, to the Army, being brought up to strength in men and equipment so that we would be in every way ready to start actual fighting. But when we told the RAF that we were mobilising and wanted to be made up to strength in RAF personnel, they professed to be quite unable to understand what we meant. They pointed out that 'the Royal Air Force had been mobilised since the day on which war was declared'. However, we got everything we wanted by operating on the DO net. In fact we got two more aircraft than we were entitled to and these came in very useful in Normandy.

RA 8 Corps dealt with the mobilisation of both my Squadron which was the Army Squadron and Evelyn's 659 Squadron which was the 8 Corps Squadron. Naturally they gave preference to the needs of their own squadron. As a result 659 Squadron was equipped with brand-new 3-ton lorries whereas we got re-conditioned lorries. This caused some bad feeling in my Squadron and there were murmurs that I ought to protest. I did nothing as I knew what would happen if I made such a protest to Hammer.

Then the BRA (Jack Parham) asked me to come to Army HQ and have lunch with him. He discussed with me all the problems which arose on mobilisation and finally asked me if there was anything he could do to help my squadron. This was a temptation which I was quite unable to resist. I mentioned the re-conditioned 3-ton lorries and the fact that 659 Squadron had been given new lorries. The BRA made no comment, but he did take action.

One evening when I was sitting in my office at Burn, Prune told me that the Corps Commander had arrived at the Mess and that he was very angry. Prune was wrong about it being the Corps Commander (it was Hammer), but he was quite right about the anger. A few moments later Hammer entered my office, sat down, thumped the table and shouted at me: Ian MacNaughton was in another room but he could hear quite clearly every word that Hammer uttered. But it was some time before I realized what he was complaining about. He accused me of having committed the appalling crime of causing trouble between senior officers. I had wondered why Hammer had come to me instead of summoning me to see him. Then I realized that he had probably just been to see the BRA at Army HQ, and had decided to give me a rocket on his way back to RA 8 Corps. I got the rocket of a lifetime but my Squadron got brand-new 3-ton lorries. So it was worthwhile.

Before ending this chapter I think I should say something about Burn which was an operational bomber station equipped with Lancasters. At that time the life expectancy of an operational bomber pilot was only a matter of weeks. I understand that each had to do thirty operational sorties before he was rested. Every night that they went on a raid over Germany a considerable proportion of them might not return: sometimes only a few returned. There were newspaper headlines of 'thousand bomber raids' but little was said of the many who did not come back. The number of bomber pilots who were killed on raids was quite appalling. They were magnificent young men and far too young to die. They had to fly for many long hours in the cold and the dark and the suspense and they must have believed that sooner or later they would go down in flames. But they were willing to do far more than their fair share of the task of winning the War.

I sensed that the Mess at Burn was a sad place. The bomber pilots were warm and friendly and yet quiet and withdrawn and not prone to the happy laughter which we had become accustomed to at other RAF stations. Their CO, Wilkinson, was an outstanding man. I admired him immensely and I thought him worthy to command those men who were serving under him. I heard a report that he had been killed shortly after we were there but I hope it was not true.

I think it was Wilkinson who told me that he had heard that one or more of my Air OP pilots had been angling for a lift, as a passenger, on a bombing raid. This sounds incredible to me as I write this but I expect that I was at the time not in the least surprised. In fact I think I myself would probably have liked to have gone one night to experience dicing with death in a bomber – but only for one night! And only if I had felt that I was doing a useful job: a mere passenger would have been of no help at all. At any rate I made it quite clear that this could not possibly be allowed. I could not explain to either the RAF or the Army how I lost an Air OP pilot in a bombing raid over Kiel!

CHAPTER XVI

Normandy

When and where the great landing on the Continent of Europe was to take place was probably the best-guarded secret of all time. All we knew was that we would be going somewhere sometime. Shortly before D-Day I received two separate envelopes: each was marked 'Top Secret'. On opening each of them I found another sealed envelope which was marked 'Top Secret: To be opened only by the Commanding Officer'.

The message in the first of these envelopes was, 'Signal estimated requirements of boiled sweets.' I replied to this on the basis of 1 lb per man. They did not bother to tell me that the recipients were being expected to pay for these boiled sweets and the bill came in after they had all been eaten. One could not expect people to pay for anything that they had already eaten in the belief that it was free and so I just sent my own cheque – sometime in July.

The message in the second of these envelopes was, 'Signal estimated requirements of prefabricated crosses.' I sent in a 'Nil return': I was not going to estimate how many of my chaps were likely to be killed. In any event it would have been bad for morale to carry our crosses with us in the 3-ton lorries and, as an Air OP squadron could make just about anything, making crosses would present no problem.

Each of my Flights went separately, at the same time as the AGRA (Army Group Royal Artillery) or division which it was to support. My SHQ Flight went last being led by a Royal Navy Walrus. It was believed that the trigger-happy Navy would shoot us down if we went without a Navy escort. In fact one ship had opened fire on the Walrus but stopped when the Walrus fired a recognition signal. I took LAC Wadhams with me on that most interesting journey from Selsey to Normandy. The sea off Normandy was crammed with what appeared to be thousands of ships. As we approached the land of France the Walrus turned for home and our four aircraft climbed up over the balloon barrage which was protecting the beaches and then dived down and began a search for the ALG which our SHQ personnel had prepared for us at the village of Banville. At first we could not find it.

Peter Kroyer had been in charge of the party which had gone by sea. He had chosen an ALG which consisted of a narrow landing strip which had been rolled flat by our 3-ton lorries in a field of growing flax. This strip was next to a small wood on the other side of which was the road in the small village of Banville, not far from the beaches.

Peter quite rightly made sure that our ALG would not be spotted by the enemy: everyone was kept hidden in the wood. No 'T' had been put out to show us where to land and there was no hint that this narrow rolled area had been flattened for the purpose of creating a landing strip – it might have been flattened by the farmer. Wadhams and I had to land in two neighbouring fields before we were told that the field of flax was meant to be our ALG. When we did land in it, we had flown for two hours ten minutes since leaving Selsey. I took a dim view of this as an Auster was said to carry only enough petrol for a two-hour flight.

That afternoon I visited my three Flights. I found that they needed several replacement aircraft. 'A' Flight was in a field at Reviers. Murray Bell had tried to protect his four aircraft from shellfire. Everyone of course slept in foxholes and Murray attempted to dig holes for his aircraft also. But this didn't work and he had had two aircraft damaged by enemy shelling. Moke Murray wanted a scythe to cut a landing strip through a hayfield.

That evening Monty and I went to call at the château in Banville. The owner was a Free French RAF Squadron Leader who had been serving in England as a fighter pilot. He was engaged in conversation with an American General who was on Eisenhower's Staff and whom I already knew well as he had stayed with my aunt at Queen Camel. The French Squadron Leader was complaining to the General that when, after the years which he had spent in England fighting for the Allies, he had at last returned home, it was to find that his daughter had been sent by Eisenhower on a 'cloak and dagger mission' behind the German front line. So Monty and I stole silently away. That night we slept, or rather tried to sleep, in a ditch beside the road. I was at a bend in the road and all that night our tanks came down that road from the beaches and just as each tank, travelling without lights, sounded as if it was about to go over me, it turned in its tracks and went round the corner.

When we had left England I had still been under Hammer's command but I had no idea as to under whose command I was now supposed to be. I went and saw Hammer and he ordered me to send pilots back to England to fetch four replacement aircraft. I decided to go myself and take three pilots with me. We flew from Cherbourg on the 30th of June in an Anson which was packed with RAF pilots who were on the same errand. We landed at Redhill and as our Austers were to be collected from Bognor, I had an excellent excuse to spend that night with Diana and Vivien (our daughter), who had had to leave their flat in London because of an unexploded bomb in a neighbouring flat, and were in a cottage on the outskirts of Esher.

That night was not a peaceful one. A constant procession of flying bombs were passing above us on their way to a neighbouring armaments factory and their engines kept on stopping sooner than the Germans had intended. As a result we kept on hearing an engine stop and later an explosion nearby.

At Bognor we found that the new Austers had not been fitted with trays for our wireless sets. Our Flights in Normandy would not have thanked us if they had to make and fit such trays. So we flew to Old Sarum where we persuaded the OTU Engineer Officer, the ever-kind F/O Poile, to make and fit them as quickly as possible: he borrowed them from OTU aircraft and fitted them in an hour or two. I persuaded the Group Captain in command of the station to give us the 'station scythe', and Monty and I flew back to Normandy the following morning. I wonder if Moke Murray's Flight in fact ever scythed a landing strip in a hayfield: it must have been very hard work.

We found that in our absence SHQ had moved to St Gabriel to a suitable field for an ALG. Geoffrey's 653 Squadron SHQ came to a neighbouring cornfield where they had to flatten a landing strip. Geoffrey's Squadron were under the command of RA 12 Corps. The demand for Air OP Flights exceeded the supply and both the CBO (Counter Battery Officer) 12 Corps and 3 AGRA needed us. So Geoffrey and Coles (one of his pilots) joined us in forming a Flight to support both RA 12 Corps and 3 AGRA. I never learned whether I was then officially under command of the BRA, or 12 Corps, or 3 AGRA. I was delighted at not being still under the command of Hammer. This Flight was surplus to our establishment, but this did not worry us at all. There was so much work to be done that I borrowed Jimmy Magrath from Moke Murray's Flight so as to give us the benefit of his operational experience in North Africa.

73

One morning I awoke to find that the night's rain had caused my foxhole to fill with water so that I was absolutely soaked; and so were we all. The next night we slept on top of the ground but the following night we were badly bombed and two aircraft were damaged and one destroyed. The ground crews repaired the damaged aircraft in a matter of hours. After that we always slept in foxholes.

While we were in Normandy the days seemed far too long and the nights far too short. At least one of our aircraft had to be in the air over the front line from shortly before dawn until an hour after sunset. The infantry regarded the Air OP as the 'orderly officer' who had to be continuously on duty above them. Even if visibility was so bad that a pilot could not identify any target, he had to just keep on flying up and down the front line. The infantry said that the mere presence of an Auster discouraged enemy mortars from firing for fear that they might be spotted.

As soon as a pilot reached the front line he found plenty going on. He would probably be welcomed on arrival by at least one enemy machine-gun firing tracer. If he was fairly low, this tracer resembled a line of red dashes zig-zagging up towards him in a vicious manner but if he was up high this tracer appeared to be coming up slowly and like a firework display. There were times when it was some seconds before I realized that it was aimed at me. I wondered why the enemy machine-gunner was wasting his time and ammunition on me when there were so many important things for him to shoot at on the ground. I somehow assumed that my aircraft would never be hit, but this is not to say that I did not take evasive action.

The drill was to pin-point on the map the offending machine-gunner, get back a bit, climb up to a suitable height though no higher than necessary and then put down a sufficient number of rounds on top of him in order to destroy him and thereby teach his friends the lesson that it was dangerous to fire at an Air OP aircraft.

Then one would approach the front line again and look for another and more important target. From time to time one might see our own or enemy fighters but they were usually some way above and too busy watching each other to bother much with us. If they did come down to worry us, our own troops below would discourage them from pressing an attack.

By about the middle of July 1944, the Germans seemed to have learned never to move by day unless it was necessary in an attack and not to fire at an Air OP aircraft unless they were confident of hitting it. This made our task more difficult. We would fly up to the front line and then up and down it and yet see absolutely nothing except an apparently deserted countryside. We could then edge further and further forward until an enemy gun decided that it could not miss and so opened fire. There was obviously very little future in this procedure though I know that Oliver Murphy habitually adopted it. I have little doubt that Oliver would not have survived the War if he had not later become the Army Commander's personal pilot – and he was lucky to survive that.

Or we could climb up high and whilst controlling the stick with our knees or as best we could, search diligently for the very faint flashes of enemy guns or for the tiny plumes of smoke which arose from enemy mortars when they were firing. One needed an observer for this as one was much too pre-occupied to be able to watch out for enemy fighters. We were equipped with chest parachutes but these were pointless as there was no prospect of an observer baling out and even if it were possible for a pilot to bale out it was unthinkable that he should do so and leave his observer to crash in flames. Whenever I did take a parachute with me, I flew alone.

I had taken a small personal radio with me to Normandy. There was a Canadian radio station which transmitted from England to the troops in Normandy. A Canadian girl with a lovely voice which was always brimming over with merriment was the announcer. She gave her name as Charmian Sansom. Her voice and the music which she presented were quite gorgeous. I particularly remember listening to Massenet's 'Meditation from Thais' which was broadcast at a time when I needed to be calmed, soothed and inspired. Fortunately the horrible screams which are broadcast now forty years on were unknown in those days. I cannot believe that such allegedly 'popular' music would have been any inspiration to anyone during intervals between dicing with death.

In fairness to Hammer, I think I should mention that he was a very competent senior gunner officer. I believe he was one of the originators of the 'stonk'. Artillery officers had all been trained to range and only fire for effect when they had got on to their target. This meant that, as soon as the first ranging round had fallen, the enemy could get into their foxholes where they would be fairly safe from the later fire for effect. A 'stonk' was a massive concentration of medium and field artillery and sometimes of heavy artillery also, which was put down on the target without any prior ranging. The advantage of this was that it caught the enemy when they were still in the open and killed them before they had had any opportunity to take cover.

As I write this I am remembering a day in Holland when Murray Bell and I were standing together in a field talking. Nearby was a road along an embankment and here the road was blocked by two dead horses and their horse-drawn vehicle. There was a ditch near to where we were standing. The enemy were not far down that road. A single shell was coming towards us: its trajectory reminded me of a golf ball being driven by a driver. We paused in our conversation for a few seconds and then, when we realized that it was not going to fall near us, we went on talking. But we both glanced at the nearby ditch. Likewise we ignored the next approaching shell. But as soon as we heard the third shell coming, we both dived into that ditch. I mention this incident as it illustrates the value of a stonk. But a stonk was of course very extravagant in ammunition.

When searching for, or actually engaging a target, we had to learn to concentrate on the job without being unduly distracted by all the unfriendly noises that we heard from time to time. There were many different types of unfriendly noises and I will try to describe each of those which I particularly remember. Whenever our own guns fired directly below us, the sound seemed to come up and strike the aircraft: this was entirely innocuous. Then there were disturbing and indefinable noises which I used to attribute to our own shells passing a bit too close. Then there was a sound as if the engine had backfired: that I believe was enemy small arms fire passing very close. Then there was a terrible sound like hailstones of steel falling on a corrugated iron roof: that I think was enemy 20 mm cannon fire and I always instinctively took evasive action. Then there was a very loud bang which shook the aircraft and I hurriedly looked round to see what, if any, damage had been done. I would then see, fairly near, a puff of smoke which had come from an enemy 88 mm gun. Whenever an 88 mm shell burst fairly close, one's heart seemed to stop beating for a moment and one was always surprised that the aircraft had not disintegrated.

It was easy to see what was going on in our own front line. I remember a certain infantry soldier who had dug himself just below the level of the ground on a hill in Normandy. He was waving frantically to me with his trenching tool and it appeared that he was pinned down by fire from an enemy weapon pit two hundred yards or so in front of him. I flew low over him and guessed that he wanted me to take on that weapon pit. Then the machine-gun that had been worrying him opened fire on me and I evaded this by diving down the slope of the hill below a crest. From further back I climbed up, pin-pointed the target on the map and gave fire orders to the guns for a 'close target'. But I was supporting an AGRA, and their job was more putting down heavy concentrations of shells than knocking out one enemy machine-gun close to our own front line. So in due course the guns reported that they rejected this target because it was too close to our own troops. What I was able to do for that soldier almost certainly did not satisfy him but I like to think that perhaps for a few minutes he felt a little less alone.

I then climbed up and tried to find a target which was further behind the German front line and which our guns would be willing to accept. But as soon as I began to observe through field-glasses, an enemy 88 mm gun opened up at me and seemed to be quite determined to get me however many rounds of ammunition it might cost. And I could not pinpoint where he was. This particular gun began to get its bursts alarmingly close to me and again and again I had to discontinue observing and save myself by diving and climbing and twisting and turning.

I noticed a squadron of our tanks stationary below me, their crews out of the tanks, brewing tea and watching my discomfiture with interest. It is always interesting watching someone else being shelled. On one of my dives I passed just over these tanks and at that moment the enemy gun got a burst beneath me and very near the tanks. I can remember being rather amused at the sight of those tank crews bundling at top speed into their tanks: none of them appeared to have been hit. I made for home to inspect the damage. I think we got that enemy gun in the evening.

I have told this story because it illustrates the point that Air OP pilots had to spend long hours every day dicing with death over the front line looking for targets which were sometimes extremely difficult to find. Just consider the strain on the nerves of the observer.

I was never shot down, whereas some Air OP pilots who were shot down survived. In September 1944, when 'A' Flight were supporting 15 Scottish Division in their bridgehead across the Albert Canal, a cannon shell exploded in the cockpit just behind Jimmy Storie and did very extensive damage to the aircraft. Yet he landed safely even though the aircraft was beyond repair and could never be flown again. When I inspected the damaged aircraft I could not understand why Jimmy had not been killed. A pilot of another squadron had a 5.5-inch shell through his rudder without exploding or altering the trim of his aircraft. In Normandy, Charles McCorry was once engaged in an operational sortie when his aircraft was hit by splinters from an 88 mm shell which put his wireless set out of action. He returned to his ALG, changed the wireless set and then continued his sortie.

Dusk sorties were as a rule more rewarding than those done by day. By day we had one aircraft on the CCRA's frequency and one on the AGRA frequency. At dusk both of these aircraft were netted in to the 'Counter Battery Officer's Bombard Net' and went up some time before it was beginning to get dark. We had already become accustomed to the Normandy countryside by day and had learned to identify on our maps every village, field, orchard or wood. As it began to grow dark we would be able to see quite clearly the flashes of any enemy guns which might be firing. We would fly higher and higher on a fine night, and the darker it became the more clearly we were able to see the flashes. That was the time when we were extremely busy reporting to the CBO the map reference of every battery that was firing. And we would watch the concentrations of shells which he then put down on those batteries – after dark bursting shells were very easy to see. This would continue until it was so dark that we were no longer able to identify the hedges and orchards of the countryside and then it was time to make for home. Frequently, just as we were about to head for our ALG, a tremendous display of tracer soaring into the night sky over the front line would herald the approach of enemy bombers which were in the habit of raiding the beaches at that hour.

Our eyes had by that time become so accustomed to seeing in the dark that we had little difficulty in finding our way back to our ALG, or in landing on it by the light of two or three green hurricane lamps.

I had chosen to place my Squadron under command of RA 12 Corps who later placed me under command of 3 AGRA. As Geoffrey was commanding the 12 Corps Air OP Squadron and was also personally flying from time to time as a pilot in my SHQ Flight, we used to joke that we were each under the other's command. This sounds nonsense, but it was typical of the Air OP. Most squadron commanders had formerly been brother officers in 651 Squadron and we were all the very best of friends loyal both to the Air OP and to each other. There were no petty rivalries, no hard feelings and there never was any conflict of command. We never quarrelled and we never allowed our squadrons to quarrel.

Our ALGs had to be so far forward that they were liable to be bombed or shelled. In Normandy my SHQ was bombed on two occasions, one aircraft being destroyed and two being badly damaged. 'A' Flight had two aircraft damaged or destroyed by shelling. 'B' Flight were bombed, two gunners were killed by direct hits on their foxholes, one aircraft was destroyed and the other three were put out of action for twenty-four hours only. 'C' Flight had one aircraft damaged by shelling.

CHAPTER XVII

The Ground Crews

The pilots were all very overworked and very tired but so were all the men. The fitters and riggers of SHQ had to keep four aircraft flying in the same manner as the aircraft of a Flight and also look after two initial reserve aircraft which we had 'acquired' surplus to our establishment. The engines of all the aircraft of the Squadron had to be 'top overhauled' every forty hours and damage due to enemy action had to be repaired immediately. They fitted new props, new engines, new mainplanes and they just about rebuilt aircraft as and when necessary.

As from the 28th of July 1944, the Army Commander's aircraft had to be maintained with an exceptional degree of care and his ALG beside his caravan at Tac Army (Second Army Commander's battle HQ) had to be prepared and manned in addition to our own. After the Falaise massacre we had to move whenever Tac Army moved and this was every day or forty-eight hours. So we had to make the Tac Army ALG our SHQ ALG. This made things much easier for us and particularly for our sergeant-major who had to collect our rations without fail.

And we made the situation still more difficult for the servicing personnel by using RAF fitters and riggers as observers. Looking back on it now I wonder how so few men could have coped with such a tremendous task and how those RAF 'tradesmen' were willing and able to work continuously from first light until after dark every day. Their only 'rests' from work on the aircraft were spent dicing with death as observers over the front line. I remember Mr Easton, the Warrant Officer, saying to me that I was asking 'the impossible' of the men.

However, they certainly achieved 'the impossible' and we never had a single accident due to faulty maintenance. The Sergeant Fitter (Airframes), Sgt Darke, found the nervous strain of so much work and responsibility too much for him and though he kept on without complaining and supervised all the work with meticulous care, during the following winter he suffered a nervous breakdown and had to be sent back to England. The signallers also were extremely busy as, in addition to the wireless sets in the aircraft, two ground stations had to be manned continuously from before dawn until after dark. And the bombardier, Bdr Hicks, of the Signal Section was a keen and reliable observer.

Each of my three Flights helped, by themselves doing much of the work that would normally have been done for them by the servicing personnel of SHQ. Hard work seems to make for contented soldiers and airmen: certainly the morale of the Squadron was never as high as it was during the France/Germany Campaign. We had a magnificent lot of men and I feel proud at remembering what they did. We had come a very long way since the early days of 651 Squadron on Exercise Bumper when the pilots were deserted by their ground crews.

Whenever the Squadron had lost an aircraft, we had to send a pilot to hitch-hike a lift back to England and fetch a replacement. Our replacement aircraft were collected from Bognor and we soon learned that they were not safe to fly until they had been thoroughly overhauled by our own fitters. Ian Young got half way across the sea to Normandy with one and then noticed the oil pressure fall to practically nil. He just managed to get back to Selsey.

One replacement aircraft reached us intact and our painting expert, Cpl Oliver, painted the Second Army Shield on it as it was to be the Army Commander's personal aircraft. But on the next day its engine failed on take-off, and Ian McNaughton crashed into a tree and spent the next few days in a field hospital. However, the Air OP had learned to surmount difficulties by having recourse to the DO net, and after these two unfortunate experiences, pilots collecting replacement aircraft flew to 43 OTU and there persuaded F/O Poile to get his servicing personnel to check the airworthiness of the new aircraft as well as fit them with the necessary trays for the wireless sets. If the Air OP had not been so much like a club of which each member was always willing to help other members we would at times have been in serious difficulties.

Our observers were quite different from the observers of the First World War who observed the fire of the guns. The job of our observers was to watch out for enemy fighters so that they did not take us by surprise. Our Austers were much less manoeuvrable when carrying a passenger as well as wireless set or camera and we, therefore, often flew alone when on operational sorties. But when we had to fly high and observe through field-glasses, it was far better to be able to concentrate on our tasks and to rely on a passenger to watch out for enemy fighters.

We tried to get Higher Authority to recognize observers officially by awarding them 'half wings', aircrew leave, aircrew rations and our flying pay of two shillings per day less tax. But the RAF Higher Authority refused this request and insisted on regarding our observers as mere volunteer passengers.

Despite this miserable meanness of Higher Authority, we never lacked volunteers from either RAF or Army personnel. I cannot remember ever asking for a 'volunteer': the usual question was simply, 'Who would like to come up and dice with death with me?' Cpl Wadhams was my usual observer, but when Mr Easton (the WO) was unable to spare him, Bdr Hicks, LAC Clutterbrook and AC Griffiths frequently observed for me and Cpl Oliver, LAC Mansfield and LAC Quickenden each flew with me from time to time. The corporal in charge of the photographic section, Cpl Hazelden, frequently flew with me on photo runs when he kept an eye on the camera (which occasionally jammed) and also watched out for enemy fighters.

Furthermore, whenever an aircraft had been serviced or repaired, we always took the senior NCO, who had been in charge of the service or repair, with us on the flight test. This senior NCO was usually Sgt Harris and he regarded his job of being a passenger in flight tests as a joke: officially it was no part of his job at all. He was always cheerful.

I think it required far more courage to be an observer than to be a pilot. This is perhaps best illustrated by the fact that when a young man today drives his girl friend at tremendous speed along narrow country lanes, it is not the young man who gets frightened. When Terry Wykes was shot down near the Rhine, his observer, McNairney, died with him.

CHAPTER XVIII
Some Battles in the Neighbourhood of Caen

I understand that Montgomery had, in June 1944, sought to attract the German armour to the Caen area in order to reduce the opposition the Americans would have to face on the west of the Allied perimeter. At any rate a limited attack near Caen between the 25th and 30th of June (Operation Epsom) drew almost all the Panzer divisions to the British sector and continued to hold them there long after the city fell on the 10th of July. The battle for Caen was preceded by a massive RAF night bombing raid on the city which I watched from some high ground behind our own lines. It appeared to me that very few people and buildings in Caen could have survived this holocaust.

I was thinking of the unfortunate French civilians in Caen. Forty years later Diana and I went back to Caen and in the Abbaye des Hommes, built by William the Conqueror and in which he was interred, we found photographs of the appalling damage caused by this bombing raid. There was also an inscription which stated that most of the French civilians had fled the city and sought refuge in the fields before the raid. But many had remained and had gathered in the Abbaye des Hommes in the belief, or hope, that the Conqueror's tomb would be inviolate. I like to think that the RAF pilots who took part in the raid had been given orders to try to avoid dropping bombs on this abbey. At any rate it was not hit and the Conqueror was given the credit for this.

On the 8th of July, during the Caen battle, I did a number of counter battery sorties, but found that there was not much that I could do other than to watch. I saw a massive German artillery concentration falling among our own massed tanks, though very few of the tanks appeared to me to have been actually hit. I kept just below a large dark cloud and had LAC Wadhams with me as observer. An enemy fighter made two passes at us but Wadhams gave me adequate warning and I was able to disappear into the cloud cover. At one time our tanks were held up by a line of German 88 mm guns which had a dual anti-aircraft and anti-tank role. I tried to locate these guns but they were too well hidden in the smoke of battle.

On the 10th of July, our troops occupied Caen and the Battle of the Orne to the west of Caen began. This kept us busy, particularly at dawn and after dusk when enemy artillery flashes were visible. I did a number of shoots which I described in my log book as 'neutralization of enemy mortars seen firing'. On the 12th of July I was asked to locate thirty enemy tanks which had been seen in the neighbourhood of St Martin but I reported that what had been seen were only bushes. In this I think I was mistaken.

At 0200 hrs the Flight which I had formed out of the pilots of my Squadron HQ came under command of 3 AGRA and at 0530 hrs the ground station and aircraft were netted to the 3 AGRA frequency.

At 1110 hrs Jimmy Magrath carried out an 'M Target' on an enemy battery (13th Medium Regt), and at 1140 hrs he carried out an M Target on two enemy self-propelled guns seen firing with the same regiment. At 1550 hrs I carried out an M Target neutralizing four enemy mortars seen firing with the same regiment.

At 1705 hrs Jimmy carried out a destruction shoot on the church tower at Feuguerolles-sur-Orne at the request of the infantry who said that the enemy were using this tower as an observation post. He scored nine direct hits but the tower was seen still standing afterwards. Presumably the enemy had given up using it as an OP.

At 2010 hrs Jimmy carried out a 'Yoke Target' on an HB (hostile battery) and shortly afterwards he reported to 3 AGRA map spottings of two other HBs which were active.

On the 14th of July we provided continuous 'Auster cover' with two aircraft from 0530 hrs to 2200 hrs. Jimmy Magrath located an active enemy heavy battery and engaged it heavily with 59th Medium Regiment as a regimental target.

Coles successfully evaded a single attack from a number of Me109s, four of which were shot down over our own lines by flak. Enemy fighters were then doing a 'milk round' daily between 1300 hrs and 1430 hrs and again just after dusk. I wrote in our War Diary, 'We will endeavour to keep out of the air between these times', but of course this was not in fact practicable.

Coles had his aircraft peppered with holes when flying at 50 feet by six enemy mortar bombs bursting directly beneath him. Pilots were then told not to go below 200 feet when flying near the front line owing to the danger of blast and splinters from shells, etc bursting beneath them.

I wrote in our War Diary that day, 'The maximum AOP height of 600 feet has gone by the board: the cloud base and the pilot's discretion are now the only limits. Captain Magrath's shoot of today was observed at 2100 hrs at a distance of 15,000 yards from a height of 4,500 feet. It was interrupted once for five minutes only by the appearance of fighter-bombers who were however discouraged by our flak from delaying their more urgent journey to bomb the beaches.'

At 1130 hrs that day 43 Div reported fifteen enemy tanks north of St Martin. I took off with orders to engage as a Yoke Target. I observed through field-glasses and was satisfied that these tanks were only the bushy-topped trees which lined the Maltot–St Martin road. I was in fact mistaken. I reported movement on the main Evrecy–Eterville road near Point 112 and some enemy six-barrelled mortars. But the target was rejected by 3 AGRA as being too close to our own troops: they were prepared to put down a massive stonk and were unwilling to risk any shells falling amongst our troops. But some regiment put down red smoke on this rejected target and it was attacked shortly afterwards by two Typhoons.

My entry in our War Diary for the 15th of July was as follows:

SHQ Flight carried out continuous Auster cover from dawn to dark in order to locate as many hostile batteries as possible so that they might be destroyed, or at any rate neutralized, before Operation Greenline which was due to commence at 2030 hrs.

During the day three hostile batteries were engaged by Captain Magrath as regimental targets scale 5, and five more were located by pilots of the Flight and reported to the CBO 12 Corps as being active.

After the commencement of the battle it was impossible to see anything owing to a smokescreen combined with smoke and dust and there was no wind to clear the air.

A custom has become established of our own fighter aircraft mildly beating up Austers before crossing the front line. The Auster then, unless actually engaged on some specific task, watches the fighter go across the enemy front line with a view to taking on any AA guns that open up on him. In return several pilots have reported that Spitfires have circled them for some time and kept a fatherly eye on them. A strong sense of comradeship and co-operation has thus grown up between fighter and Air OP pilots.

I will add to this that I had called on Johnnie Johnson (a very famous fighter pilot) one day towards the end of June. He and his squadron were in an orchard beside their operational airstrip. The fighters, particularly the ones that took oblique photographs, had been suffering appalling casualties over the enemy front line. We agreed on how to help each other. Enemy light anti-aircraft guns were a bit afraid to open fire when an Auster was watching. Our observers had noticed that they and even the 88 mm anti-aircraft guns, only fired at us when our backs were turned unless they believed that we had already seen them. And we felt much more relaxed when we saw our own fighters not far away.

But once mobile warfare had begun, some of our pilots took a dim view of being 'mildly beaten up' by our own fighters.

On the 31st of December 1944, I noted in my log book that I had been twice 'attacked' by single Spitfires but I didn't mind at all as only a week before I had been chased by an Me109 and only saved by effective fire from the ground.

On the 16th of July, I wrote in the War Diary: 'The battle for Evrecy and Esquay. 658 SHQ Flight unable to do anything useful owing to low cloud, smoke and dust. Auster cover was provided as usual but flying was difficult owing to the constant necessity of dodging Spitfires, other Austers and the shells from our own guns which appeared to be tightly packed along the whole front. Flying in front of such massed guns when they are firing concentrations is very unpleasant.'

The 17th of July, was a very memorable day for me. I was awakened in my foxhole by Geoffrey Pollitt in the middle of the night. He brought with him a written order from RA 12 Corps signed by Tony Hughes-Gibb (who had been with me in the Dorset Yeomanry). It was marked 'Secret', but I don't think that matters now. I will set it out here:

1. Intelligence sources appreciate that enemy tanks are harboured in areas St Honorine-du-Fay 9557 and Avenay 9559. It is thought there are at least 40 tanks in each area.

2. The CCRA has ordered that, if the weather allows, you will send out an Air OP on 17 July as soon as it is light enough to get good observation. The Air OP will order these two targets to be engaged it he sees signs of enemy tanks in the areas. Both targets are recorded as ML 24 and ML 25 respectively by the Corps artillery of 12 Corps and 30 Corps and 2 Canadian Corps but only a proportion of the artillery can reach. The LO [liaison officer] who is bringing this will also bring you the message ordering these ML targets to be recorded and giving the necessary data. They are stonks in each case.

3. The Air OP will net in on the CCRA's command net at 0600 hrs 17 July using the code signs CSX 6. Details of the comd net are attached.

4. 30 Corps have a station on the net so they will hear the orders and co-operate accordingly. We will pass the orders to 2 Canadian Corps from here.

5. Method of engagement, etc . . .

And there was a note that the divisions and AGRA of 8 Corps had been placed under the command of 12 Corps for this operation. So we would in effect be observing for the guns of the entire 21 Army Group.

Geoffrey and I sat down and talked this Order over in the middle of the night. I had twice insisted that reported tanks were only bushes. And now Corps 'intelligence sources' were insisting that there were no less than eighty enemy tanks behind the enemy lines and on the far side of a hill which we could not possibly see over unless we went to a great height over the front line. At such a height the enemy 88 mm anti-aircraft guns just couldn't miss us and, even if they did miss, we would not be able to see tanks from such a height. It was fairly wooded country and there were so many bushes. The intelligence sources had said that the tanks were 'harboured', and the obvious place to harbour tanks was in the thickly-wooded country beside the River Orne and this was even further behind the enemy lines.

We soon came to the conclusion that the only possible way to find these tanks was to fly very low across the enemy lines. In this way we would be certain to find them – if they were really there and if we were able to get that far.

Then we discussed the question as to whether or not this order could properly be rejected on the ground that it was not within the compass of the Air OP. We had seen again and again what happened to fast German fighters who tried to fly very low over our own lines and the German Army surely couldn't miss a slow Auster flying just above their heads. But it appeared to be vital to Corps to obtain this information. An infantry officer could not, without being accused of cowardice, refuse to carry out an order just because it meant almost certain death. So nor could we. It must never be said that the Air OP lacked 'guts'.

Obviously neither of us could possibly order anyone else to do the job. Either we could draw lots as to which of us was to go; or we could both go in separate aircraft and hope that one of us might be able to send back the required information before being shot down. We decided that we would both go, that we would set off at the same time at first light, that we would both fly very low but by different routes and that our best hope was that the enemy infantry might not be early risers and that the enemy anti-aircraft guns might be avoided by such low flying. There was an obvious advantage in our both going: neither could possibly turn back when confronted with the massive concentration of fire that would come up at him from the ground.

Since we both believed that we had only a few hours to live, we did not bother to try to sleep that night. We sat and talked. Geoffrey told me of his Hungarian girl friend with whom he had been corresponding through the Red Cross (and whom he married after the War): I realised that on such occasions one feels no sense of fear – only quiet resignation.

At first light there was a thick mist and it was not even possible to see the tops of the trees. Flying was quite out of the question. It was not until about 1100 hrs that the mist began to clear and before then the order had been cancelled. Presumably intelligence sources had reported that there were no longer any tanks in either of the villages mentioned in the written order. What an anti-climax!

As from 1100 hrs that day continuous Auster cover was provided: in fact at least two Austers were always up watching the battle. Our front line was somewhere south of the road which runs from Eterville to Point 112 to Evrecy. The enemy were still holding Maltot and Avernay. South of the enemy line was a low hill, on the other side of which there is a fairly steep slope down to a tributary of the River Orne and this steep slope down was entirely invisible to both the ground troops and for all practical purposes, to the Air OP. Just the other side of the top of this hill lies the attractive village of St Martin which was visible to the Air OP but not to the ground troops. The southern part of this village is called Vieux, presumably because it is the old part of the village. It was obvious from the map that any strong counter-attack would be mounted from this village and the open country which lies to the west of it in the neighbourhood of the road which runs from St Martin to Esquay.

It had been difficult for me to see into St Martin because of the houses and the many tall trees which were then in the village. I had previously kept on observing this area through field-glasses, but thought I saw only bushes to the west of the village – they looked like stunted may trees. There were and still are, a number of such bushes, but the enemy had in fact assembled a considerable number of tanks, probably covered with camouflage nets, in this area. It is not easy to see clearly through field-glasses on a 'bumpy' day and perhaps I was unfortunate in the 'bushes' which I did examine. At any rate the fact that none of these 'bushes' ever moved had confirmed my belief that they really were bushes.

The weather was hot and dry and in those conditions in Normandy no vehicle of any size and particularly tanks could move without giving rise to a cloud of dust. So the Germans only moved under cover of darkness – unless of course they were on some particularly urgent business. I had seen no dust: all had appeared to be quiet in St Martin.

But all had certainly not been quiet in Maltot. This was not far behind the enemy front line and was obviously heavily defended by the enemy as whenever I approached it I was met by heavy fire with red tracer. To some extent one could ignore, if necessary, 22 mm and 88 mm fire, but red tracer when one was low was very difficult to ignore. This presented an added problem when I was trying to watch what was going on in the area of St Martin. It persuaded me to observe from rather higher up than I would otherwise have done.

When I went up at 1600 hrs on the 17th of July, I saw immediately that the whole of St Martin, including Vieux, and some of the open ground to the west of the village, was covered by a dense cloud of dust. I also saw that all the 'bushes' that had been south of the road from St Martin to Esquay had either disappeared or moved to join the other bushes nearer the village and to the north of this road. I could not see much through this dust, but I did vaguely see vehicles which were probably tanks moving there and I saw a German staff car emerge from the dust and halt on the road leading from St Martin to Maltot. I assumed that he had halted just before the crest so as to be just out of sight of our ground troops. An officer got out of this vehicle and looked as if he was waiting for something.

My conclusion (perhaps I should say 'guess') from what I had seen was that the tanks would soon be going over the hill and down to Point 112, and that a convoy of vehicles were getting ready to start on the journey by road down to Maltot. I immediately reported over the R/T to RA 12 Corps and recognized the voice of Tony Hughes-Gibb. After a slight pause he told me that I was going to have an 'ML Target, scale 4'. The guns were reported ready in a very few minutes. I gave the order to fire.

The whole of St Martin and Vieux disappeared in an enormous cloud of black smoke and to the west of the village there appeared to be an oil blaze. Then I moved the concentration 400 yards to the west for a repeat. I thought that no one in that area could have survived and that the roads through St Martin would have become impassable for any traffic. It was a miracle that none of our own shells had hit me *en passant*: certainly I would not have been flying where I was if I had known in advance how many shells would be passing all around me.

After I had landed, Tony asked me what my target was. This was not an easy question to answer. I was convinced that my target had been a very considerable number of tanks and I estimated their number on the basis of those already reported to be in that area. I could also have made a rough guess from the 'bushes' which had moved. But the dust had prevented me counting tanks or vehicles. So I replied, 'Forty tanks lurking under cover'.

Extract from RA 12 Corps Intelligence Summary – dated 18/2150 B was as follows:

Target engaged by OC 658 Air OP Squadron controlling all guns 12 Corps proportion guns 30 Corps and 2 Canadian Corps ● Tgt harbouring enemy Tks MT and inf demolished by tight concentrations from the Corps Artys well synchronised ● Only one correction required ● Black smoke observed from tgt area ●

Embargo has been placed by Second Army on all LAA [ie light anti-aircraft fire] more than 5,000 yds behind front line owing to incidents of engagement of friendly planes ● AOP pilots must be warned of this reduction of their defences.

I mentioned in the War Diary that 'the usual 88 mm gun south of Caen put two AA bursts unpleasantly close to the pilot during this shoot.'

This was by no means the end of that memorable day. I will continue to quote from the War Diary:

At 1900 hrs the enemy commenced shelling our gun areas and Capts Magrath and Murphy took off in an endeavour to locate the enemy guns firing. But the wind had dropped and a smoke and dust haze had made observation impossible.

Shortly afterwards the usual 88 mm gun south of Caen shot down a Typhoon returning from a raid with the very first round it fired at it. Capt Kroyer went up immediately to avenge this but though he flew at 4,500 feet over the vicinity of the gun watching hard for a flash and very much ready both to locate the flash and dodge the burst, the menace held his fire. This gun appears to make a point of only firing at an Auster when its back is turned. We have located this gun within about 500 yards and intend to knock him out as soon as we can get him a bit more accurately.

At 1920 hrs Major Pollitt, working with 658 HQ Flight, carried out a Yoke tgt with 3 AGRA on a place 500 yards NE of St Honorine where he had seen dust and movement of vehicles.

Whatever the result of the bombardment of St Martin on the 17th of July, 43 Div were obviously delighted. So much so that the following day they asked me to do the same to Maltot despite the fact that this was not very far from their own front line. This I did with all the guns of both 3 and 9 AGRAs in two 'Yoke Targets'. The enemy in Maltot must have been quite shattered by the devastation of St Martin behind them on their line of communication and the subsequent devastation of Maltot must have been the last straw. At any rate 43 Div then occupied Maltot and our line moved forward.

My attention was then switched to another part of the 12 Corps front and on the 20th of July I observed a 3 AGRA concentration put down on thirty enemy mortars at Rocquancourt. That day I noted that I had watched an enemy barrage going down and that it had missed all our concentrated tanks.

On the 18th of July an incident occurred which is, I think, worth recording here. I will describe it as I wrote of it in the War Diary:

Big attack (the breakthrough we hope) begun in a SE direction via the east of Caen by 1 and 8 Corps with 7, 11 and Guards Armd Divs under Comd. Meanwhile SHQ Flight continues to support 3 AGRA.

Owing to heavy aircraft casualties among 653 AOP Squadron, SHQ Flight 658 Sqn now provide two aircraft daily on the CCRA 12 Corps Comd net and one aircraft on 3 AGRA AOP net.

Captain Kroyer took off at 0700 hrs in an endeavour to locate the 88 mm gun or guns south of Caen by seeing their flashes during the big bombing raid and was returning from a successful sortie when he saw a Spitfire coming down in flames about a mile SW of Tilly-sur-Seuilles and a parachute descending nearby at 832652 in the area of the front line. Observing from about 3,000 feet he noticed that the pilot was working his parachute while descending but afterwards lay on the ground apparently unconscious.

Believing the pilot to be wounded and in danger of capture by the enemy and seeing a man running with the pilot's parachute into a nearby wood, Captain Kroyer wondered whether this running man was a German soldier or French civilian. Captain Kroyer descended to 500 feet but was unable to identify the running man, though he did see the parachute lying at the edge of the wood and he noticed that the pilot was now lying with one leg bare as though his trousers had been partly removed.

Realising that the field in which the Spitfire pilot was lying was either near or inside the German lines, Capt Kroyer decided to land and pick the pilot up in order to prevent him being captured and so that his wounds might be attended to immediately. Visibility was very bad owing to smoke and the ground in the vicinity was pockmarked with shell craters. He decided to land on a level ploughed strip, considering the risk of soft plough to be less than firmer ground pitted with craters. The aircraft, however, dug into the plough on touching down and turned over on its back.

Capt Kroyer and his observer LAC Griffiths climbed out and hurried to a nearby British Infantry Carrier Platoon which they had noticed from the air. They borrowed a carrier and bren gun from the platoon and set out for the spot where the pilot had come down. A forward section of the DLI eventually stopped them and warned them that the enemy were 100 yards further down the path. They then endeavoured to approach by another route but were discouraged by enemy fire.

Capt Kroyer then went to a forward platoon HQ where a major of the DLI showed him on a vertical air photo the enemy's dispositions. From this it was clear that the pilot had fallen some distance behind the enemy lines, close to a German Company HQ.

This major said that it would be useless to try and reach the spot in a carrier as the intervening ground was under fire and the distance too great. He did however, promise that if our advance continued to the field where the pilot lay, he would search the neighbouring wood and farm for him. Capt Kroyer then went forward some way on foot, but, coming under fire again, he decided to return to the SHQ ALG and report. In the afternoon he carried out a recce from 1,500 feet and saw that both pilot and parachute had disappeared.

Now what is an Air OP squadron commander going to do when one of his pilots goes on such a frolic of his own? We were always short of aircraft and pilots and I had to send Ian Young back to England to fetch another aircraft. Or perhaps I sent Peter Kroyer – I forget. I have referred to the hazards involved in fetching replacement aircraft from England. Peter's frolic was rather like that carried out by Charles Ballyn at about the same time but I intend to write a separate chapter about Charles Ballyn later on. I did not know whether to give Peter a rocket or to praise him. I certainly admired his courage, but it was stupid of him to have attempted to land on a ploughed field.

In fact the AOC 83 Group, Harry Broadhurst, personally sent a message warmly thanking

Peter. As I have already said, Group was always kind and understanding. The Royal Air Force may not have understood the Air OP but they did understand pilots.

I have set out above at very considerable length a mere six days in the history of a Squadron HQ Flight which was no part of our establishment and which would never have existed at all had it not been for the fact that there was such an urgent need for our services. Perhaps I should add that every pilot on SHQ was very keen to enjoy operational experience. We had Peter Kroyer, Monty, Oliver Murphy and Ian Young and I had borrowed Jimmy Magrath from 'C' Flight to help us.

Jimmy did a wonderful job and I wish I had been able to get him a Bar to his DFC for what he did in Normandy. But the CRA took the view that this would be premature and then Jimmy flew into some HT cables near Vimoutiers. His aircraft was destroyed but he was physically unhurt and was able to hitch-hike back to our ALG. However, his nerve was obviously affected, as usually happens after such experiences and for some time afterwards he appeared to be very much on edge. After the battles of Normandy were over, I returned him to 'C' Flight where he did excellent work during the rest of the War.

Considering the time it has taken me to record some of the experiences of only one Flight during a mere six days, it is obvious that it would be quite impossible to record all the innumerable experiences of my entire Squadron during the France/Germany Campaign which lasted nine months.

I selected those particular six days, not because they were an exceptionally eventful time, but because in the book *Unarmed into Battle* there is a paragraph as follows:

> Larger and larger concentrations of guns were turned on to important targets and on the 17th of July 1944, Major Lyell, CO of 658 Squadron, conducted a shoot on forty enemy tanks lurking under cover; in this the artillery of 12th, 30th and 2nd Canadian Corps with their supporting Army Groups RA, say some five or six hundred guns of field, medium and heavy artillery, participated. This was possibly the largest 'battery' directly controlled by one man – certainly by a pilot flying a light aeroplane.

An obvious question arose from this 'lurking under cover': if they were 'under cover' how could I have counted them? I think the answer to this question will be reasonably clear from what I have set out above. It is possible that Geoffrey's 'Yoke Target' later that evening dealt with the remaining forty tanks.

Shortly after the concentrations on St Martin and Maltot, I heard a report (probably from an ADC to the Army Commander) that these had broken up an enemy counter-attack and that it was believed that they had sustained fifty per cent casualties. I then wondered how anyone our side of the lines could possibly know this and I assumed that it was just an unfounded rumour. But many years later I read a book called *Ultra in the West: The Normandy Campaign of 1944–45*, written by Ralph Bennet. From this it appeared that, unknown to junior officers such as myself, a group of code-breakers in a hut in Bletchley Park had been decoding with amazing speed radio messages sent by German generals to their High Command and forwarding them immediately to the Allied High Command in Normandy. There were 25,000 or more such signals based on the Bletchley decodes. I will quote only three of them which may be relevant to my story.

> Soon after Operation Goodwood opened on 18th July, 1 SS Pz captured a map from a British aircraft which force-landed just South of Caen but there was no indication that it gave away anything vital.

This was clearly a reference to Peter's frolic. Air OP pilots marked their maps only with targets and never took any secret documents up with them.

Allied artillery-spotter aircraft had lately been the subject of frequent complaint: on 12th July, 47 Corps and 2 Pz Division grumbled that they were 'overhead the whole time' – only to be silenced by Jagdkorps II's rejoinder that it could only operate at the most vital spots and that Army Group 'B' had ordered it to concentrate its main effort on another part of the front. This was evidently East of the R. Orne, for soon Panzer-gruppe West, 86 Corps and 21 Pz Division all combined to proclaim themselves 'thrilled and grateful' for support recently received. Bouquets like this had not often come the German Air Force's way since the landings but there were two more in the same week. Air patrols were said to have reduced the army's losses of motor transport and at nightfall on 17th July 10 SS Pz Division reported 'great joy' in its ranks at that day's raid by Flieger Korps IX which had kept the enemy's artillery quiet for twenty minutes (!)

Possibly the most useful piece of information from Ultra during the 48 hours of severe fighting was the news that due West of Caen 16 GAF Field Division had been so badly smashed by 19th July that what was left of it had been taken over by 21 Pz Division which had itself had to give ground the previous evening after at first making some progress with a counter-attack.

This last piece of information could only have referred to 43 Div and Operation Greenline. 'Due West' of Caen was in fact well behind our own front line: Operation Greenline was south-west of Caen along the road running from Eterville to Evrecy, whereas Operation Goodwood was east of the River Orne and south of Caen.

Today at Point 112 stands a monument erected 'To the memory of all Ranks of the 43rd (Wessex) Division who laid down their lives in the cause of freedom June 1944 to May 1945. This memorial is erected on the site of the First Major Battle in which the Division took part July 10th to July 29th 1944 when this Ridge, Château de Fontaine, Eterville and Maltot were captured and held.'

Since the War, I have often worried about the unfortunate French inhabitants of the villages of Normandy. This inspired me to visit these villages forty years after they had been destroyed in the process of being liberated. Normandy had to pay a very high price in lives and property for liberation. Diana and I visited many of these villages including St Martin, Maltot and Evrecy.

In St Martin and Vieux, the church has been restored and the rest of the village has been entirely rebuilt with houses which are quite lovely and with gardens of which the owners can be proud. New houses are now in course of being built to the west of the village. The Norman architects who designed all the houses for all classes of people in the countryside of Normandy after the War did a magnificent job. How I wish we had had such architects in Britain.

I spent some time in the graveyard on each side of the church, reading the inscriptions on all the gravestones. It was not at all as I had feared. There was indeed one stone which recorded the deaths of six or seven members of the same family as 'civilian casualties' in the 'bombardment in the cause of freedom'. This stone got the date of the bombardment entirely wrong and this suggested to me that by the date of the bombardment almost all the French villagers had left and the village had been taken over by German troops. In this event it is unlikely that the villagers would have returned before about the middle of August. However, there were two other gravestones for individuals with a similar inscription though on these the date was correct.

I was delighted to see at the southern entrance to the village a prominent notice which displayed a Union Jack and stated that the village had been 'twinned' with another in Devon. This surely made it clear that the villagers felt no bitterness towards the Wessex Division.

Maltot and Evrecy also contained only houses which had been built since the War. The church in Evrecy had been completely rebuilt but I did notice that cracks had already appeared in two of the stone pillars. The graveyard by the church likewise contained very few graves of French civilians killed in July 1944. Obviously the civilians here also had left their homes before their town was destroyed.

CHAPTER XIX
Falaise

About the 20th of August 1944, my SHQ were using as an ALG a field nearby to the ancient Norman castle of Tornabu. Beside this field was a small orchard where we were all encamped. On the other side of this field was a clump of trees and to the highest of these a German eagle had been attached. I assumed that this was some form of booby-trap and gave strict orders that no one was to climb that tree in order to collect the eagle as a souvenir.

The field and some buildings nearby contained a considerable number of German dead and these we had to bury. It was a nasty business but it had to be done. At that time the whole countryside was littered with dead Germans and I saw several of them who appeared to be little more than children. Hitler was clearly short of soldiers and had begun to obtain recruits from the schools. I saw one dead boy who appeared to have knocked out a Churchill tank before he died at his gun with a bullet through his brain. The Germans were certainly heroic soldiers who kept on fighting after all was lost.

That evening Oliver Murphy returned after dark from the Army Commander's ALG, and I remember wondering how on earth he had made the cross-country flight on such a dark night. He landed as usual by the faint light of two green hurricane lamps.

Not long afterwards we heard a German bomber fly over us and it dropped a parachute magnesium flare which lit up with a dazzling brightness our ALG and the adjoining orchard in which we were camped. The bomber could scarcely fail to notice our four or five picketed aircraft. I shouted to everyone to get into their foxholes, but I am sure that no one required any such instructions from me. It was quite obvious that we were about to be bombed.

As the flare came slowly down, I thought how nice it would be if I could get hold of a number of such flares so that we could use them for observing the enemy front line after dark. I could perhaps use Monty's windscreen wiper beam to guide me.

We heard the bomber enter a shallow dive towards us and then came the whistling sound of a stick of bombs coming down. I wished my foxhole had been deeper and I lay at the bottom face down and hoped for the best. Our foxholes were all fairly close to each other and the stick of bombs landed in a straight line right down the middle of them. I think there were six or seven bombs but two of them failed to explode. They were probably about 50 lb bombs.

The sensation was almost identical to that of receiving six strokes of the cane at school. One counted each stroke and longed for the last one, though the bombs succeeded each other a bit faster than the strokes of a cane had done. One bomb landed about six feet on one side of my foxhole but it did not explode. The next one landed about ten feet the other side of me and did explode. The next, and last, bomb fell just the other side of the hedge beside a picketed aircraft but did not explode. Then the flare went out, the enemy bomber made for home and the air in our orchard was filled with the stink of the exploded bombs.

I got up expecting to find that a considerable number of us had been killed, but to my amazement I discovered that no one had even been hurt. It appeared that an occupant of a foxhole was safe unless a bomb landed directly on him. So that German pilot had done a magnificent bit of bombing and yet had achieved nothing. He had certainly taught us the value of foxholes. Of course if the bomb which had fallen beside the aircraft had exploded, we would have lost that aircraft. I don't know what would have happened if the bomb which landed about six feet from me had exploded: if it had, I very much doubt that I would be writing this now.

After the massacre at Falaise, I flew over the scene to have a look. But when I saw one of the aircraft of my Squadron which had landed in a stubble field and broken its prop against a cornstook, I landed beside it to find out what it was doing there.

What I found beside the road nearby was one of the most terrible sights that I ever saw. The least mobile part of the German Army had been trapped when they were trying to escape before the Falaise Gap was closed. Hitler's orders that they were not to retreat had caused them to delay too long before attempting to escape. They had been heavily shelled by the Allied artillery and heavily attacked by our aircraft.

There was a multitude of dead, dying and wounded. Dead horses lay where they had fallen. Dead cattle were everywhere in the surrounding fields. German transport blocked the road. Our medical equipment was temporarily unable to cope with so many wounded. I have never discovered why so many of the vehicles were covered with swastika flags. I still have one such flag that I collected that day. I was quite appalled by the spectacle of so much suffering and misery. It had to be, and we then believed that it heralded the end of the War. But I found it hard to feel any pleasure in that victory.

Many German soldiers had kept dogs as pets and these dogs remained beside the bodies of their masters until they were buried and then ran wild. Some were adopted by British units. 'A' Flight acquired an adorable spaniel which remained with them at any rate until after the end of the War: it always gave me a warm welcome when I visited them.

CHAPTER XX
Communication Flying

On the 27th of July 1944, Dickie Dawson, one of the Army Commander's two ADCs, came to our ALG and said that we were to fly the Army Commander, General Sir Miles Dempsey, the following day from the field beside his caravan at Cairon to a field beside the Commander-in-Chief's caravan the other side of the battle front and back again. It was only about thirty miles each way, but the Normandy roads were then so congested that it might have been a day's journey by road. I thought this flight would be an isolated incident and so decided to do the job myself. I had no wish to be responsible by proxy for the Army Commander's death and, if I had to accept responsibility for his safety, I preferred to die with him.

The following day I arrived a few minutes early at the field at Cairon: it was a large and easy grass field. The Commander arrived punctually and so I did not have to switch off. As soon as we were airborne he produced a map and followed our route on it, asking me from time to time the names of villages over which we passed. It occurred to me that he was taking no chances of my getting lost. Within twenty-five minutes we reached Montgomery's field.

Now the C-in-C was flown by an RAF pilot in a Miles aircraft which had a very much better performance than the Auster. In fact I had tested the Miles prototype about two years before when I was an instructor at Larkhill. I had then recommended that the Miles should be adopted for the Air OP because, not only was it a beautiful aircraft to fly, but it could be landed in and taken off from fields surrounded by trees which would be too difficult for an Auster. However, it had been decided that the Auster had other, and more important, advantages over the Miles in that it could be much more easily repaired after damage as a result either of an accident or enemy action. So this Miles prototype aircraft was the only Miles AOP aircraft which existed.

On this occasion I found that the C-in-C's field was surrounded by trees but I decided that I could just get into it. It was one of the trickiest landings that I ever did and I think the Commander recognized the difficulty as he asked me if I thought I could get out of it again. I replied that I would prefer to take off alone and find a more suitable field for taking off with him. This I did and a few hours later I flew him back to Cairon.

When we arrived there he told me that he had decided that this was obviously the best way for him to get about and that I was to provide him with a regular pilot who would be available at all times during daylight to take him wherever he wanted to go. So I arranged that Ian McNaughton, my squadron captain, should become the Army Commander's pilot.

Our duties to our three flights and our commitments to 3 AGRA made it extremely difficult for us to provide the Army Commander's aircraft and to maintain an ALG next to Tac Army. There he had three majors, Robert Priestley, Bobbie Morrison and Bertie Hesmond-Halgh, and two or three captains whose job was to keep him at all times completely up to date in the battle picture. There were also the necessary staff for running Tac Army and the

Commander's bodyguard. Tac Army was located not far from the front line. Some considerable distance behind it was Main Army where the Chief of Staff and his staff lived. And many miles behind that was Rear Army: I never went there and I'm not sure what they did: presumably everything that was not needed for fighting battles. We became proud to belong to Tac Army.

Tac Army was constantly moving and in hilly country it was often difficult to find a suitable field beside the Commander's caravan. On the other hand we could cut down trees and borrow from the Engineers a grader to level a landing strip. On one occasion the grader levelled a narrow strip on the top of a hill, but the Engineers omitted to cut down an apple tree beside the strip. Ian omitted to do a dummy run, made a low tactical approach and only saw the apple tree when it was too late to avoid it: one wing of the aircraft knocked the tree down and there was resulting damage to the aircraft. The Commander accepted this mishap without comment and I sent a ground party who replaced a mainplane of the aircraft within a few hours.

A few days later we received a new aircraft from England and not then knowing that new aircraft were unreliable, we allotted it to the Commander and went to a great deal of trouble painting the Second Army shield on it. Fortunately I had told Ian always to test every field by himself before taking the Commander off from it, and so he was alone when the engine failed shortly after take-off and he crashed into a tree. He was taken to hospital and an order was sent to me to send another aircraft and pilot immediately. This order passed through RA 12 Corps who decided to instruct their own Air OP Squadron to comply with the order.

The pilot sent was not very experienced and the Commander subsequently said that from the moment of take-off he suffered acutely from 'anxiety neurosis'. When they arrived at 30 Corps ALG they found that this was a very narrow bulldozed strip and that the soil that had been removed had been heaped on each side of the strip. There was a very strong cross-wind and it would require great skill to land without drift and to keep the aircraft straight after touching down. I understand that the pilot went round again twice and then landed with more determination than skill and failed to keep the aircraft on the strip. As a result of hitting the heap of soil on one side of the strip, the aircraft came to rest upside-down. It was a terribly serious matter at the time, but later it became an Air OP joke that we all had to learn the correct method of saluting an Army Commander when he was upside-down.

This sort of thing simply could not be allowed to happen and the following day all Air OP Squadron Commanders of Second Army (Evelyn Prendergast, Alec Hill, Geoffrey Pollitt and I) were summoned by the BRA to Main Army where the following rules were laid down:

1. The Army Squadron would be responsible for the Army ALGs and the Corps Squadrons would be responsible for the Corps ALGs.
2. All ALGs which were likely to be used for communication flying would be at all times properly manned and marked out and absolutely safe and easy for use.
3. If any accident were to occur in the future, if it should be shown to have been due to the fault of the pilot, then the squadron commander who had provided that pilot would have to take full responsibility. On the other hand, if the accident was due to a too difficult ALG, then the squadron commander responsible for the ALG would be blamed.

This could only mean that if there were to be another accident, at least one squadron commander would be broken.

At the time we thought these orders were unreasonable, but soon we realized how very wise they were. We had previously rather taken pride in the difficulty of our ALGs. From that day onwards it ceased to be possible to justify an unnecessarily difficult ALG on operational grounds and from then until the end of hostilities in Europe no pilot of my Squadron was involved in any accident when carrying a passenger and no pilot of any other squadron had any accident on one of our ALGs. And I believe the other three squadrons had the same accident-free record.

Perhaps I should qualify this statement. When we were in Belgium we had posted to us a Belgian Squadron Leader so that he might learn all about the Air OP. He was very popular with all of us. But no RAF officer, whatever his flying experience with the RAF, could be expected to be able to land in, or take off out of, our operational ALGs, nor could he be expected to be able to conduct Air OP shoots – unless of course he had been fully trained by our Air OP OTU.

I sent this Belgium Squadron Leader to Murray Bell's 'A' Flight, but Murray soon asked me to take him back to SHQ on the ground that he was not fit to conduct shoots. One day I had to provide a pilot and aircraft to fly a Tac Army officer to Ralph Cobley's ALG on the outskirts of Antwerp. Ralph's 652 Squadron were supporting the Canadian Army and Ralph may not have known of the instructions given to us by the BRA of our Second Army.

The Squadron Leader did an RAF-type landing at Antwerp and the 'float' caused the aircraft to overshoot the ALG and crash into some tents. This did only minor damage to the air-. craft, and I sent a party to Antwerp to repair it and fly it home. But unfortunately Ralph had sent an accident signal to the Air Ministry and this led to my receiving repeated demands from them for an accident report.

I realized that if I had to send in an accident report, I would have to put all the blame on the Higher Authority which had sent an untrained pilot to serve as an Air OP pilot. This would have stirred up a hornets' nest as the RAF Higher Authority refused to believe that Air OP flying required any special skills.

In fact the RAF had even had the bright idea of 'resting' fighter pilots in a 'Communication Flight' which had so many accidents that soon no Army officer would fly with them, and the Army Commander had issued an order 'Fly Arty and be safe.' (Before the War, Imperial Airways had advertised 'Fly British and be safe'.)

I had recourse to the 'DO net' to persuade the Air Ministry that they would have to do without an accident report. The Group AVM, Harry Broadhurst, was always most helpful.

As Ian had been somewhat shaken by his accident, I had to find another pilot for the Commander. I chose Oliver Murphy because he was not only a brilliant pilot but also the sort of person who would not be alarmed by anything. And so, on the 22nd of August 1944, Oliver became pilot-cum-ADC to General Sir Miles Dempsey and he remained with him until the end of hostilities in Europe, after which he went with him to the Far East and in June 1946, to the Middle East. His duties in mobile warfare were particularly arduous as the drill was that he must fly to, and land at, every ALG by himself before he flew the Commander there. Further, the Commander refused to accept the distinction which I endeavoured to draw between 'Commander's weather' and weather fit only for operational flying. If the weather was good enough for an Auster to fly, then it was good enough for him.

There were occasions in mobile warfare when very difficult ALGs *had* to be used. When Tac Army first moved to Achel in November 1944, we hurriedly prepared a temporary ALG there which was to be used only until we had prepared a better one. Whereupon it rained without ceasing for two days and the greater part of our field was covered by water several inches deep. Thanks to a strong wind we were still able to fly from this field but it was impossible to taxi without assistance and every time we took off or landed we were drenched with water. It was shortly after I had protested to Alec Hill about one of his ALGs, and I well remember his remarks after he had landed on this field at Achel and received a shower of water in the cockpit.

In February 1945, Oliver flew the Commander the 180-mile journey from Tac Army at Lille St Hubert to a conference with Eisenhower at Epernay in France. We sent a ground party to establish an intermediate ALG where the aircraft was refuelled both on the way there and on the return journey.

That evening I waited on our ALG for their return: it was always difficult for me to relax until all aircraft were safely home at night. The cloud was getting lower and lower and as it grew dark it was difficult to see the tops of the trees. But I knew that the Commander and Oliver had become used to flying in mist and storms and I suspected that they would try to get home.

We put out a flare path of green hurricane lamps and we stood by ready to fire Very cartridges as soon as we heard an Auster. But no Auster came that night. It was not until after midnight that the Commander returned to Tac Army by armoured car and I learned what had happened. After they had refuelled on the return journey, the cloud had descended until Oliver decided to get down somewhere rather than risk hitting a tree or HT cables. So he landed in a field beside a road. Unfortunately they were in the American Sector.

Now it would be easy for the British Army Commander to hitch-hike anywhere in the British Sector. But it was quite a different matter in the American Sector. Oliver, as pilot-cum-ADC had of course to be their spokesman. The first jeep he succeeded in stopping was being driven by an American sergeant who flatly refused to give them a lift, saying, 'Sorry buddy, but my Lieut wouldn't like it.' However, they got home in the end.

This incident did not deter the Commander in the least. On many occasions in Germany, when I thought the clouds were too low or the wind too strong, I respectfully suggested to him that he should not fly but should go by road instead. But he always said to Oliver, 'Let's go up and have a look.' And once they had taken off they never turned back.

On the 27th of April 1945, Oliver went to England on leave and I decided to fly the Commander during Oliver's absence. In the morning I flew him to an American Army field at Uelzen and then to 8 Corps at Lüneberg. When we were on our way back to Tac Army at Mengebostel we met a front consisting of a very black and threatening anvil-shaped cloud and a strong blustery wind. As there was obviously no way round this cloud, I flew under it. I soon noticed that the aircraft was being drawn up into the cloud and I had to throttle back and put the nose down to avoid climbing further. Then we met a wall of torrential rain and I suspected that the engine would soon fail as a result of flying under what really amounted to a waterfall. The turbulence was such that I was afraid the aircraft might break up. So I insisted on turning and flying the Commander back to Lüneberg. I remembered that Alan Gee had been killed near Doncaster in similar conditions of turbulence.

The pilots of my SHQ flew many senior British and American generals and we all found the same thing: that, once in the air, generals ceased to be generals but became friends instead. However aloof they may have been on the ground they were delightful passengers, and we soon learned to treat them as friends we were always glad to see. The explanation may be that dangers shared forge a bond between people: taking off from a muddy field or from a strip rolled by lorries across snow could be an alarming introduction to a flight.

One day I had to send a pilot and aircraft to Antwerp to fetch a general who had just arrived from England. I sent Monty to do this job. Before getting into the aircraft the general explained to Monty that he was terrified of flying, that because of this fear he had arranged to come to the Continent by sea, and that he wished a staff car had been sent for him by the Army Commander. Then he climbed into the aircraft after Monty had promised to do only gentle turns. During that flight Monty had to take evasive action round trees to escape an enemy fighter. When they reached Tac Army, Monty said something to his passenger about the enemy fighter and the general replied, 'Thank God I didn't know about it. I kept my eyes tight shut during the entire journey.' I remember General Dempsey saying that Air OP pilots didn't salute generals – they just waved goodbye to them when they parted. This was certainly what Dempsey himself did.

On the 5th of October 1944, the Army Commander and the American liaison officer at Tac Army, Major Danny Miller, needed to fly the hundred miles to the Headquarters of the First American Army at Verviers which is just north of the Ardennes. Oliver as usual flew the Commander and I flew Danny Miller. The ALG there was on the top of a hill just south of Verviers and was, in certain weather conditions, a bit of a nightmare. The unfavourable weather conditions were when the hill was shrouded in mist or when there was a strong wind blowing down the hill. The field sloped fairly steeply down the hill and it was certainly not possible to take off uphill and into wind. Taking off downwind involved getting off the ground before the hedge and then surviving the downdraft that one thereupon encountered. In short, when conditions became really bad all flying had to stop.

Oliver and I waited by our aircraft while our passengers were with General Hodges, the American Army Commander. Two Belgian girls arrived at the field on their bicycles and they came and talked with us. Had it not been for their appearance they would probably have been kept off the field for security reasons. The elder, Lydia, was aged about twenty and very pretty: and the younger, Nicolette, was aged about eighteen and extremely beautiful. They were both full of the joy of life and obviously thrilled by liberation after years of German occupation. They treated us as if we were knights in shining armour and we were naturally most gratified.

Nicolette suggested that we should land on a football field near the château where she lived and she thereupon produced a visiting card on the back of which she drew in pencil a sketch which showed the location of the château and of the football field. This she handed to me and I saw that her name was 'Nicole Speder de Harven' and her address 'chez le Vicomte de Biollez, Theux'. Theux is a village in the valley about two miles south of where we were. I had studied French literature and Roman Law at the University of Grenoble and so could carry on some sort of a conversation in French, though I probably mixed a bit of Italian with it.

That would have been the end of the matter had it not been for the fact that when the Commander came back he said that I would have to wait an hour or two before Danny Miller would be ready to go. Oliver then flew off with the Commander, leaving me to wait for my passenger. Nicolette and Lydia had left sometime before and I had nothing to do.

So I filled in the time by writing on a message pad as much as I remembered of the well-known 'Chanson de Roland' which begins,

Nicolette je te vois
Comme une petite étoile

It was one of the earliest of French poems which dated from the very beginning of the Age of Chivalry but I wrote it in modern French. I of course signed it 'Aucassin' and put it in one of the highly coloured message bags which we always carried with us, replaced the bar of lead with a bar of aircrew ration chocolate and took off on a sortie which I could describe in my log book as 'recce of alternative ALG'. I reached the château just as Nicolette and Lydia were arriving there and I came down low and dropped the message bag at Nicolette's feet. A few minutes later I was back at the American ALG to wait until Danny Miller arrived for the flight back to Tac Army. I hoped that I had given Nicolette something to remember.

Two days later Danny Miller had to go back to Verviers and I offered him a lift if he didn't mind my calling at one of my Flights on the way. At Verviers he kept me waiting a very long time. I spent some time chatting with American 'flyers' as they then called themselves and then sat in my aircraft and waited. It occurred to me that Nicolette might be unfamiliar with the 'Chansons de Roland' and might not even have heard the story of Aucassin and Nicolette. In that event she would think me completely crazy. So I amused myself while I was waiting by writing on a message pad in my best French as much of that story as I could remember:

LE VRAI HISTOIRE DE AUCASSIN ET NICOLETTE

A very long time ago there was a King of France who had an only son named Aucassin. Aucassin was trained in all knightly pursuits but he was a sad disappointment to his father because he showed no interest in feats of arms but preferred to spend his time writing poetry. And he fell very much in love with Nicolette and begged his father to give him leave to marry her.

Nicolette was young and very beautiful, virtuous and chaste. But she was not of royal birth and she was, therefore, not a suitable wife for Aucassin. So the King gave orders that Nicolette was to be confined in a castle far away and that she was never to be permitted to see Aucassin again.

Then a Moorish Army invaded France. The French King decided that he was himself too old or too sick to lead his Army into battle and so he sent for Aucassin and ordered him to take command of the Army. Aucassin said that he would only do so if his father first gave him a solemn promise that, when he had driven the Moors out of France, he would be permitted to see Nicolette once again and to kiss her two dear eyes and the tip of her beautiful nose.

The King had no alternative but to accept these terms. When the French Army met the Moorish Army, Aucassin placed himself at the head of his knights and gave the order to charge. But, as he raced at full gallop towards the enemy ranks, all his thoughts were of Nicolette and he was composing that poem which I sent you. He scarcely noticed the enemy as he crashed through their ranks. He won a great victory, but all it meant to him was that he would see Nicolette again.

Well satisfied with my French composition I put it with the remnant of my aircrew chocolate ration in a message bag, looked round to make certain that there was still no sign of Danny, swung my prop and took off. After I had done a circuit of the château, Nicolette, Lydia, their mother and their grandmother all came hurrying out on to the lawn and waved. So once again I went down low and dropped the message bag at Nicolette's feet.

The following day Danny wanted to be flown back to Verviers and again I flew him there. This time there was a mist which became steadily worse during the course of the afternoon. By the time Danny was ready to go, flying was quite out of the question. This was all right for Danny: he had plenty of friends who would find some accommodation for him for the night. I did not relish the prospect of spending a cold night sitting in my aircraft. So I started walking through the mist – in the direction of Theux. I was on my way to seek a bed for the night. I had an excellent excuse to go to the château: those two message bags were the property of the Air Ministry and I should ask for them back.

The castle had a massive door and heavy iron shutters behind every window on the lower floors. I rang the bell, but it was some time before anyone came to the door. This was understandable considering that it was dark and misty and the Germans were only two miles away. General Hodges had given advice to the local community not to put out any Allied flags in case the front line should change and the Germans return. I of course had my revolver with me and had been glad of it during my walk there.

Finally a girl called asking who was there. I gave 'Aucassin' as my password and thereafter I was left in no doubt as to the warmth of my welcome. I was easily persuaded to stay the night and soon I was enjoying a hot bath followed by an excellent dinner. The Speder de Harvens were occupying part of the castle as their own home had been destroyed by the War. The Vicomte with his wife and ten-year-old son were in the other part. The son became an ardent admirer of mine: he called me 'Monsier l'Aviateur.'

That was an evening which I will always remember. All I will say of it here is that Nicolette granted me Aucassin's due reward – to kiss her dear eyes and the tip of her beautiful nose.

My bedroom and bathroom were at the top of a spiral staircase. Throughout that night a procession of flying bombs passed overhead on their way to Liege which was obviously their target. I slept in luxurious sheets on a real bed. I got back one of the message bags but Nicolette would not part with the other as she had taken to wearing it round her waist as a belt. I was up and away at dawn, had breakfast in the American Tac Army Officers' Mess and then flew Danny back to Tac Army in brilliant sunshine.

Danny and I were stuck at Verviers for another night, this time because a strong wind had made our take-off downwind impracticable. Both girls were away at a dance in Verviers and I dined with the Vicomte and Vicomtesse. They were delightful people.

In January 1945, I had a Flight supporting the 51st Highland Division in the battle in the Ardennes. The castle was then in the front line and appeared unoccupied. As I had a camera in my aircraft, I took an aerial photo of it surrounded by all the evidence of battle. I sent this photo to Nicolette as a Christmas card in December 1945. I still have her reply. She had married a Frenchman in August 1945. She said that she would always keep the photograph as a 'splendide souvenir de guerre' and would in due course show it to her children to whom she would sing the beautiful story of the valorous Aucassin.

The original story of Aucassin and Nicolette ended sadly and so did this one. In 1947 I received a funeral card edged in black informing me that Nicolette had been killed in a motor accident in France – and that she had left a daughter aged one.

I have kept as souvenirs of Nicolette her visiting card on which she had sketched the castle and the football field, and her Christmas card. Also a little green toy monkey which she gave me saying that it had been her dearest possession as a child, and that, as long as I kept it, I would be lucky and it would protect me from misfortune. I will never part with it. I have been so very lucky.

The above story will sound quite absurd today in 1985, when the word 'chivalry' is regarded as an affront to 'women's lib'. What an enormous gulf exists between the days of 1944 and now.

I was not the only pilot who flew Danny Miller to General Hodges' Headquarters at Verviers. Monty flew him there one day and had a very different kind of adventure. After

Danny had finished his task there he came hurrying back to the aircraft and told Monty that a raid by American bombers on Aachen was due to take place in a few minutes, and he asked Monty to fly him in that direction so that they might watch the raid. But as they were passing over Verviers bombs were falling all around them. The American bomber pilots had mistaken Verviers for Aachen. It was hoped that the unfortunate Belgian inhabitants of Verviers believed that the bombers were German.

CHAPTER XXI
Liberation

In 1944 the word 'liberation' was synonymous with destruction. For example, when we left Normandy the town of Evrecy was a heap of rubble under which countless dead lay unburied. The stench of death was such that it was intolerable to fly over either Evrecy or Falaise even at 1,000 feet. We hoped that these dead were mostly Germans.

But it was very different once we had broken out of Normandy. Then we were a victorious Allied Army chasing a defeated German Army and we did not expect to stop until we reached Berlin. It has been very rare in history that a defeated Army in full flight ever stopped and fought again. We did this at El Alamein and the Germans did it at Arnhem, but this says a great deal for the courage and fighting spirit of both our nations.

I had said goodbye to 3 AGRA and moved my SHQ landing strip to Tac Army and from then until the end of the War my Squadron Headquarters' ALG was always as near as possible to the Army Commander's caravan.

The Commander wisely gave the French Armoured Division the privilege and pleasure of liberating Paris. The Americans were to share this task with them. The rest of us were to liberate Brussels but this was to be merely an incident on our journey to Berlin. My 'B' Flight were to go with 30 Corps and my SHQ would of course go with the Army Commander. The other two Flights as well as most of the Air OP were to be left beside the Seine with the artillery until they were needed. It was not long before they were all needed again.

No members of a victorious army like being left behind and so deprived of the pleasures of liberation. I understand that a pilot of another squadron flew to Paris to have a look at the liberation there but arrived about two days too early. His aircraft was damaged by enemy 88 mm fire and he forced landed in a street near the centre of Paris. He got down successfully but the Germans killed him as he was getting out of the aircraft. Later the French decorated his burnt-out Auster with wreaths of flowers.

At about the same time the CCRA 8 Corps (Hammer) got the commander of the 8 Corps Air OP Squadron (Evelyn Prendergast) to fly him to Paris to have a look at the liberation. They were unaware that a German Panzer Division was still in woods somewhere near Paris, until they were flying low over these woods. As soon as they heard the sound of small arms fire coming up at them, Evelyn took evasive action and got down to just above the ground. Then bullets started coming through the aircraft all around them. Evelyn received a blow on the back of his neck from flying perspex. Then Hammer suddenly bent down and clutched his leg, and, as he did so, a bullet passed by where his head had been a second before. Hammer exclaimed, 'I've been hit': a bullet had passed through the calf of one of his legs. Evelyn somewhat tactlessly replied, 'Thank God it was you and not me', meaning thereby that, as he was at that moment doing a steep turn a few feet above the ground, if he had been wounded they would have flown into the ground and both would have been killed.

But their aircraft had been very severely damaged, and Evelyn had the utmost difficulty in keeping it flying. However, he managed to pull up over another small wood and to get to some open country where there were no more Germans. Soon he realized that he must get down somewhere before the aircraft broke up completely. So, when he saw an American Airfield Construction Unit working on repairs to a disused airfield which was pock-marked with bomb craters, he crash landed there.

The Americans rendered first aid to Hammer's wound and then sent them off home in a jeep. After they had gone some considerable distance they met the leading tanks of the French Armoured Division which was on its way to liberate Paris. As they were able to tell the French precisely where the enemy were, their journey was after all not entirely unnecessary.

Some officers of my 'A' Flight set off in a jeep to see Paris while it was being liberated. On their way there they were ordered by an American military policeman to turn into a field beside the road and they obeyed. An hour later they asked the American how long he intended to keep them there. He replied that his orders were that no British were to be allowed on the road to Paris and that any British vehicles that came along were to be put in that field and left there. So they made a plan and successfully diverted the American's attention long enough to enable them to resume their journey.

On the 26th of August, when I was flying to Gacé, a Dakota flew past me and I noticed that the flag of France had been painted on it. I assumed that it was flying General de Gaulle towards Paris.

On the following day I flew a Brigadier Webb from Gacé to an ALG near the River Seine. The direction of the wind necessitated going in low to land over a long line of guns which were firing on some task across the river. It was a noisy business, but I took care not to get too far in front of the guns and so stop one of the shells. My passenger did not seem to be in the least alarmed. He was a delightful passenger and I was very sorry to hear shortly afterwards that he had been killed by a mine.

The real hero of the Seine crossing was a German infantryman who, with a rifle fitted with telescopic sights, killed no less than thirteen of our sappers who were attempting to get a bridge across the river. From time to time our artillery put down a considerable number of rounds to kill him or drive him away, but each time a British soldier appeared on the opposite bank, the solitary German rifleman killed him. Our artillery got him in the end but he had held up the crossing of the Seine by many hours. One cannot but feel the greatest respect for a soldier who, when ultimate defeat was inevitable, fought on alone until he was killed.

After we had crossed the Seine we were welcomed by the French inhabitants of every village through which we passed. There were triumphal arches made of flowers and gifts of eggs and fruit to every soldier. And the French Resistance were most helpful. One Air OP officer when travelling in a jeep ran into a party of Germans who opened fire, killed his driver, and pinned him down in the ditch into which he had jumped. His only weapon was a revolver. However, a party of the French Resistance arrived opportunely and soon killed all the Germans.

It was difficult for us, who had never known hate, to understand the hate exhibited by the Fench towards their countrymen who had collaborated with the Germans. In many French villages ceremonies took place at this time during which women 'collaborators' had all the hair shaved off their heads and were then stripped naked and forced to walk through jeering crowds.

When we were at Thilliers en Vexin for two nights the Commander's caravan was in the grounds of a château and our ALG was a stubble field just outside the gate. The

Commander's bodyguard mounted a guard on the gate. A number of evil-looking civilians with rifles arrived and requested admittance to the château so that they might kill its occupants who, they said, were collaborators. They were refused admittance on the ground that the Commander must not be disturbed.

The occupants of that château in fact appeared to be very civilised people. One of our airmen who was an excellent pianist had been given permission by them to play their grand piano whenever he wished. We suspected that it might be a case of the village communists wanting to kill the local gentry. This of course was really no concern of ours and as soon as we had moved on the next day, these gentry were presumably murdered. This seemed very sad.

The following day I had a most unusual communication job to do. Major-General Hobart (known as 'Hobo') had come to see the Commander and I was asked to fly him to the Canadian Army (Main) HQ. My job was unusual in that we had all been moving so fast that Hobo had no idea as to where the Canadian Army HQ was. It was a lovely sunny day and we had a delightful treasure hunt landing in fields all over the countryside until we eventually found our destination which turned out to be in a wood on the south bank of the River Seine near Caudebec. Fortunately he had brought a picnic lunch with him and this was enough for both of us.

During the picnic lunch in an orchard we discussed the fact (which Montgomery had not yet learned) that courage is an expendable commodity. Hobo said that the heroic 7th Armoured Division had had their heroism somewhat blunted by their battles in North Africa and should have been given a longer rest in which to recharge their batteries of courage before they were sent to fight further battles in Normandy. He said that the 11th Armoured Division, which was perfect in every way, had shown themselves to be far better than the 'Desert Rats' during the Normandy battles. I later learned that Hobo had trained the 11th Armoured Division and that he was said to be the leading expert on tank warfare during the War. He had come out of retirement at Churchill's request and had raised and trained the 79th (Specialized) Armoured Division and had designed the new weapons which they used: the 'Flails' which blew paths through minefields; the 'Crocodiles' which scorched our enemy with liquid fire, and the 'Buffaloes' which swam ashore on to the Normandy bridgehead.

I have presumed to say that Montgomery had not yet learned this lesson, because Montgomery always placed his finest divisions in the forefront of every battle and foremost among these were of course the 51st Highland and the 15th Scottish. Not long after the War, I met an elderly general who insisted that Montgomery had done great harm to the people of Scotland. To be fair to Montgomery, it must be said that the Scots were magnificent soldiers and his paramount aim was to win battles.

This fact as to the expendability of courage was something which the RAF and the Air OP had learned from experience. Any pilot who had had a nasty experience needed to be rested.

On the day on which the Guards Armoured Division and my 'B' Flight arrived in Brussels, the Army Commander moved to Blairville where we found an ALG which would have been perfectly safe had it not been for the fact that it was necessary to climb over some HT cables after taking off. Normally we would have been quite willing to accept this risk, but my orders had been to ensure that every ALG used for communication flying should be safe. So I sent Ian Young to approach the local authority and enquire whether they would be willing to take down the HT cables. They did so forthwith and without protest. Shortly afterwards we had visits to our ALG by all the Corps Commanders.

The following day I was given the job of flying Lt-General Sir Frederick Browning, the

Terry Wykes and Tony Knight after they had landed at Brussels on the 4th of September 1944.

Terry Wykes with one of the two Belgian Officers who welcomed them at Brussels airfield.

Commander of the 1st British Airborne Corps, from Tac Army to Amiens Airfield, whence he was to fly by Dakota back to England. I did not then know it but he had just been briefed as to the planned airborne drop which was intended to secure the advance of our Army through Nijmegen to Arnhem. It was, therefore, of the utmost importance that he should arrive safely in England. I decided to do this job myself.

There was a strong wind and we arrived at Amiens in a hailstorm. A squadron, or possibly several squadrons, of Dakotas arrived at the same time as we did. They were bringing urgently needed supplies of petrol for the Army. I got into the circuit and awaited my turn to land on the runway but it soon became clear that I wasn't going to get a turn. The Dakotas treated my little Auster as being of no importance and landed one after the other as if I wasn't there. Further, they were all firing red Very lights as they went round the circuit and I assumed that this meant that they were short of fuel and anxious to land as quickly as possible. As they were travelling much faster than I was, there was a considerable risk of one of them colliding with my Auster.

There was an area of grass behind the Watch Office but there was a great deal of junk parked on this: it looked like mines or bombs. However, the wind was so strong that I decided to land just behind the Watch Office and between the piles of mines or bombs. I landed successfully and as my distinguished passenger was getting our of the aircraft I received a rocket from an indignant duty pilot for having landed there. My passenger stood up for me and insisted that I really had had no alternative.

The next day we moved on to an ALG beside a château at Perek on the eastern outskirts of Brussels. That afternoon most of us drove through the town in order to sample the joys of the liberation of that lovely city. All, or almost all, of the inhabitants were lining the streets and were giving the British Army a reception similar to a Roman 'Triumph'. We drove in a jeep at what was no more than a walking pace, shaking hands with innumerable civilians, receiving presents of comice pears and bunches of grapes and feeling that this was one of the really great days of our lives. We British felt that we were admired and loved as never before in our country's history.

Later that afternoon I walked alone through the streets of Brussels. A nun stopped me and told me that she urgently needed help. A German soldier had thrown a stick grenade from the street through the window of a school: it had failed to explode and it lay in the centre of a large schoolroom. She had cleared the school and she needed someone to render the bomb safe and then remove it.

Bomb disposal was not my line but a sapper soldier happened to be passing at that moment and so I asked him to help. I felt that I could scarcely remain with the nun and the children outside the school while the sapper diced with death inside, so I sat on the floor beside him and watched him at work. It was very interesting and a new experience for me. I think a sapper requires a very special brand of courage.

That evening many of us returned again to the centre of Brussels. We found that no one would take any money from the British troops: everything was free, including travelling on the trams. As soon as we entered a bar, we were picked up by beautiful Belgian girls who had assumed the job of entertaining us and when we attempted to pay for our drinks, the management insisted that there was no charge.

Ian McNaughton and I spent that evening touring Brussels with two lovely Belgian girls who were probably only seventeen or eighteen years of age. One of them told me that her father was an importer of wine from Burgundy. At 2200 hrs she became rather agitated and said that she must hurry home and, as this did not seem to be an occasion on which the book of rules should be followed, we drove her to her home in my staff car. On the way she said, 'My father will beat me': I wonder if Belgian fathers still beat their daughters.

We stayed at Brussels for seven days waiting for the rest of our Army to catch up with us and for the supplies of fuel, food and ammunition that would be necessary for us to continue on our intended journey to Berlin. I, as a squadron commander, had a particularly anxious time trying to keep all members of my SHQ out of trouble. They were all having the time of their lives and we then thought that the War was almost over. It would probably soon have ended had it not been for the extraordinary decision of the politicians to insist on unconditional surrender by the Germans. That absurd decision enabled Hitler to fight on until the bitter end. Surely we should have just announced that our task was to liberate Germany from Hitler and his thugs.

Even while we were still in Brussels we had quite a number of flying duties to perform every day. I see from my log book that I flew four or five sorties each day. And all the aircraft had to be serviced or overhauled in preparation for the next advance. We managed to acquire through RAF channels enough tents to get everyone under cover.

I had sent a pilot back to England from Gacé to fetch a replacement aircraft. On his way back to us he had followed the axis of advance of the British Army, but had experienced considerable difficulty in locating our ALG. One evening he was forced down by low cloud and he landed south of Brussels on the field of the battle of Waterloo. He taxied up to a farmhouse on the outskirts of a village, switched off, and asked the farmer if he would be willing to put him up for the night. The farmer received him with great friendliness and introduced him to a girl of about twenty who happened to be staying at the farm: perhaps she had been sent there by her parents so as to get her out of Brussels during any fighting that might have taken place there. At any rate she was not the farmer's daughter.

After they had had supper, the farmer announced that their guest would sleep that night with this girl. The girl appeared to be somewhat shaken by this announcement, but did not argue the point. When they went to her bedroom that night she told him, while she was undressing, that she had never done anything like this before, that she was a virgin, that she was engaged to be married and that she was very worried as to what her future husband would say when he found that she had already lost her virginity. The officer assured her that he would respect her wishes. He turned his back on her and went to sleep, so he said. He awoke in the morning to fine her fully dressed. She said simply 'Merci', kissed him on the lips and left him.

Another officer was picked up in Brussels by an attractive girl who took him to what he believed to be her home. To his surprise and delight she took him into a very large sitting room in one corner of which was a bed. He was surprised at her having such a palatial bed-sitting room and delighted with the obvious opportunity provided by the bed.

She did not appear to be particularly shy as she forthwith invited him to undress her. He accepted this invitation with alacrity but as soon as she was naked she smeared oil all over her body. She explained this by saying that she was about to give him a wonderful new experience. He was puzzled but he assumed that she had some fetish of which he had never previously heard.

Then she invited him to 'rape' her. There followed a tremendous struggle during the course of which he found that the oil had made her surprisingly elusive. However, he eventually got her on to the bed and she then co-operated and so enabled him to achieve his object. When he was exhausted and anxious to sleep, she insisted on his dressing and leaving as quickly as possible.

A few nights later a brother officer took him to see some of the lesser known sights of Brussels. During the course of the evening he was taken to a house which seemed familiar. They went upstairs into a room in which a number of people were gazing through peep-holes at some 'naughty spectacle'. He paid the equivalent of about ten shillings and was allotted a peep-hole which enabled him to see everything that was going on in the room below. He immediately recognized the room and the girl. Afterwards he said that it was well worth the ten shillings as he knew personally the officer with whom the girl had been performing.

I myself had no such experience in Brussels. My job was to keep everyone out of trouble and to ensure that no one was ever drunk in charge of an aircraft. It was not easy and I was glad when we moved on.

I will end this chapter by setting out Tony Knight's own story of how he and Terry Wykes arrived in Brussels at a time when some Germans were still there:

"It was the 4th of September 1944, and my 'B' Flight was close to Brussels. We were attached to 5 AGRA which was under command 30 Corps. I was ordered to try to 'occupy' Évère (the Brussels Airfield) if at all possible. An escort was to be provided for our vehicles to expedite their progress through the enthusiastic but delaying Bruxellois on the roads. After putting Charles Ballyn in charge of the ground party, I took off with Terry Wykes to carry out a reconnaissance. We made the usual 'dummy run' over the airfield and, as it appeared to be deserted, we landed and taxied up to the buildings.

Suddenly two shells landed, one about 100 yards from us and the other a bit further away. These shells appeared to have a double 'bang' and this was because the enemy were shooting at us over open sights from not far away. I immediately jumped back into the aircraft and reported over the radio to 30 Corps that we were under fire on the airfield. The Corps Commander (General Horrocks) sent a message that a squadron of armoured cars were on their way to deal with this situation.

Terry and I then decided to have a look inside the buildings. We saw two officers who were wearing dark bluish-grey uniforms complete with pilots' wings coming towards us and, assuming that they were German, we hurriedly drew our revolvers, but they called out 'Nous Sommes Belges – nous sommes vos amis – Belges – amis!'

As soon as they had seen that our aircraft was British they had put on their military uniforms and come to welcome us. They took photographs, one of Terry and me in front of the aircraft, and then one of each of us with one of them. Later I received prints but lost the one of me with the Belgian, but retained the other two.

They invited us to go that evening to 'La Maison des Ailes', the Wings Club of Brussels. I later discovered that membership of this Club was restricted to those who had fought in the air against the enemy. These two officers had done this in the First World War. We of course had to decline their invitation. The Flight ground party were already arriving and there was much for us to do. So we exchanged names and shook hands and bade our new Belgian friends 'Au revoir'.

The other aircraft of the Flight landed safely, and the whole Flight settled in to our new quarters which had been so very recently occupied by the Luftwaffe. I was then summoned to the 30 Corps net radio and ordered by General Horrocks himself to report together with Terry Wykes to 'La Maison des Ailes'. I was told that a 30 Corps vehicle would be sent to take us there, and we were ordered, repeat 'ordered', to travel in this vehicle which would arrive in thirty minutes time.

LA MAISON DES AILES

A. S. B. L.

Avenue des Arts, 53, Bruxelles.

CARTE DE MEMBRE
ADHÉRENT

délivrée à

M *Captain K.A.H Knight*
658 Squadron R.A.F.

Signature du titulaire,

Knknight.

Membership card and badge of La Maison des Ailes.

The Club was a rather lovely house in a distinguished terrace in the Avenue des Arts. Our Belgian friends, who clearly in some way had influence, greeted us at the door and introduced us to many other Belgian officers, but above all to countless lovely girls.

We were then made members of the Club and given the badge to wear, together with a membership card. These I still have.

Champagne of the best marques only was served, and it appeared to be in abundant supply. Every bottle had a red diagonal overstamp reading 'Fur Wehrmacht Nur'! The language of the evening was French, which with my French background presented no problem. I tried to stay close to Terry in case he had language difficulties, only to find that he spoke French better than I did. I can clearly recall that at about 10 pm, when we had been there for between three and four hours, I was leaning on the bar and explaining, no doubt in fluent inebriated French, that the village of Aunay-Sur-Odon was reduced to dust, and to this day my last words that I can remember were something like 'Awn-er-Od, ce n'est que de la poussiere.'

The following morning, the 5th of September, I awoke in bed in the room which had been selected by my batman and which I shared with Terry. I found that I was in my pyjamas, and I had some difficulty in opening my eyes. I then noticed another bed quite close and that it was occupied by Terry. I then noticed that my clothes were on a chair at the foot of my bed all neatly folded! This was very unusual indeed. Rolling over I saw Terry's clothes similarly folded at the foot of his bed: on his forehead he had a perfect lipstick kiss and he had another across his lips. I was convulsed with laughter and this awoke Terry who, when looking at me, began to laugh also. I, too, was similarly decorated!

Clearly two of those lovely girls had brought us back to our quarters and put us to bed. We both tried to find out from our brother officers and from the men of the Flight what had happened when we had been brought back to our quarters, but they refused to say a word. Those lovely girls had somehow persuaded them to keep this a secret."

Alas, Terry was killed before we crossed the Rhine.

CHAPTER XXII
Aerial Photography

When we were in Normandy it was one of the Royal Air Force's jobs to do a daily photo run down the enemy front line. But their casualties were so appalling that the Air OP later took over this task. By that time we had, as I have already said, taught the enemy not to shoot at us unless they felt confident of being able to hit us.

We were equipped with a photographic section under Corporal Hazelden. The RAF could not possibly have sent a better man for the job. I think most people who are concerned with photography are perfectionists and Hazelden was certainly no exception. It was really due to him that the photographs which I took were consistently excellent. It was no part of his job to come flying with me at all and yet he frequently came with me to help me set the camera and to act as observer. He must have had nerves of steel. It must be far more alarming to be a passenger than the pilot.

As we had only one photographic section per squadron, this was clearly a job for me and I thoroughly enjoyed every one of the fifty-two operational photo runs that I did. Before doing a run I liked to be briefed as to precisely what the photographs were required to show. This enabled me to decide on the best height for the run and as to how oblique or vertical the photographs should be. As a rule the artillery required an oblique photo run taken from a height of between 2,000 and 2,500 feet which would show them their targets. Whereas the infantry required an oblique photo run taken from a height of between 1,000 and 2,000 feet which would show them the weapon pits of the enemy infantry who were facing them. But the higher command and the sappers would probably want also a nearly vertical run, taken from the lowest height at which I dared to fly, of any canal or river across which it was intended to build bridges. This last requirement was the most hazardous and the most exhilarating.

I had to consider the cloud base and the visibility. The most rewarding conditions were a bright sun behind me after a wet night had washed all the dust out of the air. Also conditions of snow when all enemy tracks were clearly visible. The height selected also had to take into consideration any trees or woods or hills which might require more vertical photographs. Sometimes I would do one run to take oblique photographs from perhaps 2,000 feet and then another run at from 700 to 800 feet. The height of the second run was probably influenced by the unfriendly noises which I had had to put up with during the first run.

Before taking off I would decide on 'Point A' where the run was to begin and 'Point B' where it was to end. Then I would fly low to 'Point A', climb up to the selected height and get into position over 'Point A' so that the enemy front line would be in the foreground of the photographs. Then I would set my course for the run and start the camera and the run. From then on I would have to fly straight and absolutely level and any slight adjustments to course had to be made by doing gentle flat turns – the wings had to be kept absolutely horizontal. I was far too busy watching the camera sights to be able to watch out for enemy fighters. There

One of a photo run Best to Veghel done 3rd of October 1944.

One of a photo run from Olland to Schijndel done at 800 feet on the 18th of October 1944. The factory in the centre of this photograph was very strongly held by the enemy and our artillery later had to destroy it completely.

One of a photo run done on the 3rd of February 1945 for the Army Commander. Note the Venlo Bridge which had been partially destroyed.

One of a photo run at 2,300 feet on the 14th of April 1945 of Verden taken just before the dive bombing attack by our Typhoons.

The same, six photographs later, showing the black smoke from a Typhoon which had been shot down.

was no point in my taking an observer with me on a low run: fire from our ground troops would, and did on one or two occasions, give me some warning of an approach of an enemy fighter and would discourage him from pressing any attack. But on high runs an observer was very useful, though sometimes I took a chest parachute instead.

The RAF photo runs in Normandy had all been taken from a very considerable height, and, as I have said, their casualties had been appalling. But we had been so successful in teaching the enemy not to fire at Air OP aircraft, that I felt that I must learn from experience how low I could fly before the enemy felt confident that they could hit me. I felt like a pheasant flying straight down a line of guns. There was some consolation in the fact that enemy 88 mm guns did not appear to be very good at hitting low birds.

On these runs I did my utmost to ignore all unfriendly noises, but I must admit that there were occasions when the worst of all of them, the sound of hailstones of steel falling on a corrugated iron roof, proved too much for me, and I took immediate evasive action by doing a spiral dive away from the enemy, getting down to below tree-top level, and giving my nerves a few minutes' rest after which I had to go back to 'Point A' and start the run all over again.

It was all rather thrilling and it did not last too long. Once I had reached 'Point B' I could stop the camera and make for home. An hour or two later a large number of sets of photographs would be rushed by a D/R (motorcycle despatch rider) to the customers and my D/R never once lost his way.

My best customer for photographs was the CRA 51st Highland Division, Jerry Shiel, who had been the chief instructor at the battery commanders' course which I had been to at Ilkley. He was particularly keen on my doing about three successive runs for the Division at perhaps 2,000 feet, then 1,400 feet and finally 700 feet. But I had quite a number of other customers. I see from my log book that on the 9th of November 1944, I did three runs at 2,000 feet, 1,800 feet, and 1,100 feet and sent off within an hour or two '120 complete sets for 12 Corps battle'. Assuming that there were at least forty-five photographs in each set, this must have been a tremendous task for my photographic section to develop. There was to be a set for each infantry platoon commander. The Air OP had moved a very long way from the original idea that our only job was to be to observe the fire of our artillery. We certainly could not have done this low photography if the enemy had known that we were taking photographs. Presumably they thought that I was just the 'orderly officer' hanging about the front line and looking for targets to engage.

Personally I believe that it required more courage to hang about for hours looking for targets, than to do a photo run and then go home.

Once only on a photo run did I encounter the enemy flak that had caused the casualties among the RAF photographic aircraft. This was on the 14th of April 1945, when David Cover flew in to Tac Army ALG and brought me an urgent request by the Commander of 12 Corps for an immediate photo run of their front line which was required for a conference to be held that evening when the attack across the River Weser at Verden was to be planned: it was to take place at dawn the following morning. There were three different roads across the river there and the three bridges had been destroyed by the enemy. My photo run was to be a fairly long one so as to show alternative routes, if any, across the river.

I took off immediately and began the run at about 2,000 feet. The evening sun was shining and it was perfect photographic weather. I had Corporal Hazelden with me. The enemy countryside appeared to be completely deserted. But as we approached Verden we saw a squadron of Typhoons coming in to make a rocket attack. As time was short I decided to go

One of a photo run done at 700 feet of the Afwaterings kanaal on the 2nd of November 1944 for the sappers.

A concentration camp near Vught twenty-one photographs later on the same photo run. I had assumed that our own troops held the ground up to the canal, but severe unfriendly noises at this point convinced me that this camp had not yet been liberated. I subsequently visited the camp.

A Tac Army ALG in the evening sun after a light fall of snow.

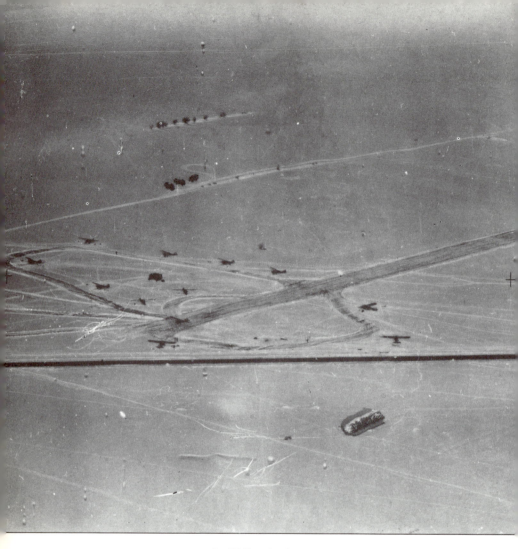

An ALG under deep snow.

Tracks in deep snow made nonsense of camouflage.

straight on and leave it to them to avoid colliding with me. As we entered the midst of them a tremendous barrage of flak came up all around us, and one of them was shot down in flames.

The flak and the black smoke from the burning aircraft made rather a mess of one or two of my photographs, but there was no time to bother about that and I went on to the end of the run. David Cover had waited at our ALG for the photographs and, as soon as they had been developed, he flew them to his Corps Commander and they arrived in time. I think this incident illustrates the measure of our success in teaching the enemy that Austers were dangerous aircraft to shoot at.

Incidentally the Corps Commander was apparently so impressed by the flak shown on the photographs that a few days later I found that I had got an 'immediate immediate' award of the DFC. The Army Commander invited me to lunch with him to congratulate me on this decoration. I was given to understand that the photo run had in fact been of great value to 12 Corps.

At the end of the War, I made some enquiries as to whether it would be possible for me to secure the award of the DFM to both Cpl Wadhams and Cpl Hazelden. They had shared so many of my dangers and surely deserved to be decorated as much as any pilot. But the difficulties were insurmountable. Firstly, each Flight would be expected to put forward the names of two of their observers. Secondly, when an RAF bomber pilot was awarded the DFC, this certainly did not mean that each member of his crew was decorated also. Thirdly, the RAF had insisted on regarding our observers as mere volunteer passengers.

From Brussels to the Rhine

After the joys of the liberation of Brussels, fighting was resumed when the Army crossed the Albert Canal and made a dash for Arnhem via Nijmegen. The Commander had to be kept informed as to how his Army was progressing through enemy-held territory on a front the width of one road. Allied gliders had already landed at certain places along our axis of advance and paratroops had secured the bridges in order to protect them from demolition by the enemy.

It was a very hazardous plan but was well worth the risk involved as, if it had succeeded, it would have probably shortened the War by six months. People who have written about it nearly forty years on and who were not there, may be unable to understand our euphoria at that time. We were chasing a beaten German Army, we were quite invincible and nothing could stop us until we reached Berlin. In any event there had, on the 20th of July, been an attempt by the German Army on Hitler's life and surely they would succeed in killing him as soon as we had crossed the Rhine. We did not then realize the evil that the absurd requirement of unconditional surrender was going to do.

On the 20th of September 1944, I took Cpl Wadhams with me and flew to Nijmegen where General Browning's (1st) Airborne Corps HQ was. I flew just over the poplar trees which lined the road. It was an uneventful flight, the Army's vehicles were moving continuously below and were spaced correctly. No hold-ups were to be tolerated and any vehicle which did break down was to be pushed into the ditch so as to leave the road unblocked. The Army had to be got, with all possible speed, to Nijmegen and then across the Rhine at Arnhem.

At Nijmegen, I called on General Browning to see if he had any messages for the Army Commander. He told me that our tanks had been held up between Nijmegen and Arnhem but that it was still hoped that they would be able to force their way through. He asked me to wait, as he wanted me to take a very important letter back with me. I was hoping that any hour we would hear that our armour had broken through to the bridge at Arnhem.

I thought that while we were waiting for this news Wadhams and I might as well fly north towards Arnhem and see what was happening. We did not get very far. There appeared to be more enemy fighters than our own and flying low in order to avoid them merely invited unfriendly noises. There was no point in our getting ourselves killed when there was that 'very important letter' to be taken back to Tac Army at Bourg Leopold. This letter was in fact addressed to Daphne du Maurier Browning. I was a great admirer of Daphne du Maurier, but I had been unaware that she was married to the Airborne Corps Commander.

When in Nijmegen that day we saw a number of German soldiers and some 'collaborators' being rounded up by the Dutch Resistance. The Resistance were certainly a great help to us in many ways.

On our way back to Bourg Leopold, a German 88 mm gun fired a few shots at us when we were over St Oedenrode. These guns were not very accurate when firing on a low trajectory. I wondered how far away it was because I could see a POW cage in St Oedenrode which contained a very large number of German soldiers who had been taken prisoner. I felt it would be unfortunate if an enemy counter-attack there were to release them all.

I reported to the Army Commander and he questioned me closely as to everything I had seen: he was most anxious that the column should keep moving up the axis of advance. That evening I took Dickie Dawson, one of the Commander's ADCs, to Nijmegen and back. We were able to report that there were still no halts in the column and apart from that 88 mm at Oedenrode, there was no sign of any enemy counter-attack on that vital road.

The following day I flew back to Nijmegen in the early morning. I flew alone as I was determined to get to Arnhem somehow and find out what was going on there and I thought it better not to take anyone with me. After calling in at Airborne Corps HQ, I set off in a northerly direction on a sortie which I described in my log book as 'Recce North of Rhine and return'. It was an exciting sortie and I was lucky to return. I did not get to Arnhem. On my way back to Bourg Leopold, I watched what appeared to be the beginnings of a German counter-attack on or near St Oedenrode and this I reported to the Commander. It must have been a worrying time for him.

The following day I took Wadhams with me and set off once more for Nijmegen. I was getting to know that road rather well. I was not in the least surprised when that 88 mm opened up at me at St Oedenrode but I wondered why the entire column had come to a halt. A little further on, at Uden, I saw Germans on the road setting fire to our vehicles. I immediately did a steep turn, climbed up a bit and had a good look to see what exactly was going on. It was obvious that a German counter-attack had succeeded in cutting the road between Uden and Veghel and that our packed vehicles were being destroyed. In a field to the left of the road there were many German dead and this showed that our troops were fighting back despite the fact that they were heavily outnumbered. A lot more of our infantry were urgently required at that point. I did not see any enemy tanks. I reported this to the Army Commander.

That same day, and at about the same time as I was there, Charles McCorry of 'B' Flight was flying a Major Hazell from Nijmegen to Tac Army with an urgent message that supplies that had been badly needed by our troops at Arnhem had been dropped into German hands. Mac's aircraft was shot down near Uden. I arrived on the scene not long afterwards and from what I saw I was able to reconstruct what had almost certainly happened. After he had been shot down, Mac had got the first aid kit from the back of the aircraft and had been in the act of administering morphia to his passenger when they were both killed by enemy fire. It was typical of Mac to attend to his passenger instead of attempting to save himself.

At about the same time James Stunt with the BRA (Brigadier Jack Parham) and Harry Salter with the Chief of Staff Second Army were flying north along that road and were also heavily engaged by 20 mm and small arms fire between Uden and Veghel. James and the BRA managed to get through with only minor damage to their aircraft. But Harry's aircraft was so severely damaged that he had to crash land a few hundred yards from the wreck of Mac's aircraft: fortunately neither he nor his passenger was wounded.

In athletics held at Old Sarum during the summer of 1943 Harry had distinguished himself as a sprinter but on this occasion he had of course to keep with his passenger. The Chief of Staff sat in a ditch and burned his secret documents with a cigarette lighter, before he and Harry, guided by a Dutch farmer, made their way safely back to our lines.

This put an end to our hope that the War would soon be over. The Flights went back to their normal task of observing for the artillery and I resumed my own task of photo runs. We had to clear all the enemy out of our side of the River Maas, get across the Siegfried Line and then prepare for the battle of the crossing of the Rhine. The war went on and on. Every day was crowded with excitement and activity. The days became weeks and the weeks became months. We had to fly whatever the weather and it was a bitterly cold winter with quite a bit of snow. Our hardships were as nothing compared with those endured by the infantry.

When the weather became really bad the Commander and Tac Army went into billets and so of course did we. Some brigadier made the mistake of ordering us to vacate our billets immediately because he required them for his own chaps. A word from us to an ADC, and that brigadier was sent packing. Two of the billets which we were occupying had the Nazi swastika painted over the entrance door. We assumed that this intimated that the daughters there had been a bit too friendly with the previous German occupants but we asked no questions. While we were in their houses retribution was postponed, but I later heard that these girls had had their hair shaved off after we had moved on.

In another village where we were billeted for a short time, my officers of SHQ and I were invited to dine with the mayor – or whatever he was called. It was a memorable occasion. It was a banquet of about a dozen different courses all of which were absolutely delicious. Unfortunately we were not warned at the beginning what was to come and long before we got to an enormous glass bowl of trifle, with the Second Army Shield in icing of the appropriate colours on top, we felt we could eat no more. But courtesy required that we should do so – and so we did. The Dutch are famous for their hospitality.

At that dinner I was placed next to a slim and gorgeous blonde who told me of her exploits when serving with the Dutch Resistance. Her task had been to carry messages which she did on her bicycle. Anyone else would have been questioned and searched by German soldiers at road blocks and other places, but her beauty ensured that she would be merely 'chatted up'.

At Lille St Hubert the Commander was billeted in a house one side of the canal, and we were billeted, and our ALG was, on the other side. The bridge over the canal had been destroyed by the retreating Germans, but the villagers organized a ferry over the canal for us. After the War there was a ceremony in the village in which this road was named after General Dempsey.

When the snow on our ALG became too deep for flying, the Engineers were ordered to level it to our satisfaction with a grader. The result was excellent until it began to thaw, after which taking off became a hair-raising experience. But the Commander's nerves were adequate for such trials. It would then have been almost impossible for him to have travelled by road. In such conditions I sent the D/R who delivered my photo runs by jeep, or delivered them myself by air.

As the months went by, I could see signs of the nervous strain to which the pilots of my Squadron were being subjected. Despite the appalling conditions of their ALGs, they had to hang about over the front line for hours every day looking for targets while our own shells were passing all around their aircraft. I can remember a day when I visited 'A' Flight and the pilots told me that they would do one more battle and that after that they would have had enough. In fact of course they went on and on until the end of the War. I think it was the RAF aircrew leave of one week in every six weeks (if they could be spared) which kept them going.

In about December 1944, 'C' Flight lost Ray Hill. He had been sent up to try to locate some enemy six-barrelled mortars near Venraij, when his aircraft received a direct hit from a shell. I do not know whether it was an enemy shell or one of our own. At any rate there was not very much left. When WO Easton and I arrived on the scene shortly afterwards, enemy mortar bombs were falling rather too close to us for comfort and another Auster of the Flight was overhead engaging them. The 'orderly officer' was still on the job.

When Air OP pilots were killed in action, they had to be replaced by pilots who had just finished their training in England. They reported to me at my SHQ and I tested them and usually found that they were not yet fit to land at the Flight ALGs. So I had to give them further instruction in short landings in cross-winds in aircraft which of course had no dual control.

On the 18th of December 1944, I decided that one such pilot was ready to join 'C' Flight to replace Ray Hill. That morning I sat beside the new pilot, gave him the map reference of 'C' Flight's ALG, and told him to fly there. Then I folded my arms and hoped for the best. When we reached the ALG it became clear that a strong cross-wind would make landing there a very tricky business. It would be necessary to come in between two haystacks and then land on a short and very narrow rolled strip which was marked by white tapes on each side and had been cleared in an enemy minefield. It we were to leave the strip on landing, we would get into the soft ground of the uncleared part of the minefield. Moke later told me that six men had already been killed in that minefield.

My pilot, whose name was Mackie, did the usual dummy run in order to learn of the difficulties and he then attempted to land. At his first two attempts I told him to go round again because his drift was wrong, but at his third attempt he made a perfect landing but then failed to keep the aircraft straight with his brakes. As we entered the minefield he braked too strongly and the aircraft eventually came to rest in the soft ground on its nose with the tail pointing straight up in the air. Fortunately he had remembered to switch off in time so that the engine was not damaged.

Under the circumstances I would have understood entirely if the ground crews had left us to extricate ourselves from our dilemma. But, without a moment's hesitation, they came running to our aid, righted the aircraft and pulled it backwards on to safe ground. Moke was entitled to be very proud of his men.

On the 2nd of November I did a series of photo runs the full length of the Afwaterings-kanaal for the CRA 51st Highland Division. Some were to be for the artillery, some for the infantry and the very low ones for the sappers. As I have said, that CRA was my best customer and I was determined that they should be perfect runs.

There were three problems. The first was that it was a very long run. The second was that there were far too many enemy firing at me from the other side of the canal. The third was that it was a day of alternate sunshine and cloud and I, being a bit of a perfectionist, wanted each run to be in bright sunshine throughout its whole length.

That day I did four runs altogether and they took me four hours of flying time, partly because of passing clouds and partly because of the effect of excessively unfriendly noises on my nerves. On my last run at 700 feet I decided that I would in no event allow myself to be interrupted again. This was taken in bright sunshine. Because of the low height required, I did these runs alone.

It was on one of these photo runs that I first saw a concentration camp. I resolved to go and have a look at it as soon as it had been liberated. I never made a note of its name, but it was in Holland and near Vught.

As soon as our troops had crossed the canal and liberated the concentration camp, Ian Young and I went there. The Dutch civilians, who had taken over the camp, received us with great courtesy and showed us round. But they did not take us into the building where the former German guards were being confined. They spoke of these guards as sadistic lunatics who could not really be regarded as human beings. From what we saw we could understand precisely what they meant. We were shown the gas chamber and the adjoining incinerator and were told terrible stories of women and children who had fought to avoid going into the gas chamber and who had thereupon been burnt alive in the incinerator. There were a number of gallows which were so low that it was obvious that the victims died from slow strangulation while their feet were only a few inches above the ground. The evidence of floggings completed the terrible picture of sadistic insanity.

Tony Knight, who commanded 'B' Flight, lost three of his four pilots that winter. Mac was killed at Uden. Charles Ballyn was mortally wounded over the Siegfried Line. During the Battle of the Crossing of the Rhine, Peter Wykes (his mother called him 'Peter' though most of us called him 'Terry': I don't know why) went up to try to neutralize some enemy self-propelled guns somewhere to the east of Rees. The smoke and haze of battle necessitated his flying over his target, whilst vast numbers of our own shells were continuously passing all around him. He was having to fly in conditions of unmitigated hell, but his duty to the infantry was imperative. His aircraft received a direct hit and he and MacNairney, his observer, were buried side by side in a little orchard close to where they fell.

In about October 1944, we had delivered to us a number of sheets of armour plate which we were to fit under the aircraft seats. The theory was that these would protect our bottoms from small arms fire. This seemed an excellent idea, but we feared that the additional weight would materially affect the performance of the aircraft, and that a crash landing might damage our backs. We had heard that a pilot of another squadron had sustained a fractured spine as a result of an armoured seat.

Before deciding whether or not to fit them, we thought it wise to test their effectiveness. So we propped one of them up against a hedge and I fired a rifle bullet at it from a distance of about sixty yards. The bullet went straight through the armour and killed a horse two fields away. This was most embarrassing. In Britain we would have given the farmer a certificate which would have enabled him to obtain compensation. But we knew of no such arrangement on the Continent. Fortunately for us an enemy fighter machine-gunned the neighbourhood later that evening and the farmer attributed the loss of his horse to enemy action. Needless to say we never fitted those armoured seats.

Tetley Tetley-Jones, who had been for a time my Flight Commander in 651 Squadron, had subsequently raised and commanded 653 Squadron. In January 1944, he had made the mistake of applying to be sent on a course for Army Lt-Colonels. This resulted in Geoffrey being given his Squadron and Tetley becoming unemployed. In the early spring of 1945, Tetley, by then reduced to the rank of captain, was languishing in a re-inforcement camp far behind the front line. He wrote to me appealing for my help. I immediately sent a jeep to fetch him and sent him to 'B' Flight where I knew he would get on well with Tony Knight. He was to fill the gap caused by the death of Peter Wykes. I then informed Higher Authority of what I had done.

This was all most irregular, but the Air OP could do such things and get away with it. Tetley did well during the Battle of the Crossing of the Rhine and we were all very glad to have him. After the War Tetley's name became very well known for his Tea Bags.

As the Army Squadron we did some unusual jobs. On the 18th of November I took up a sergeant of the Army Film Unit to take photos for 'Movietone News'. And from time to time we took up wireless operators who were experts in receiving coded messages in the morse code from 'cloak and dagger' agents in or just behind the enemy front line. One day I sent

Ian Young up to do this job in a snowstorm which became so bad after he had taken off that I feared that he would never find his way back to our ALG. We had no windscreen wipers. But to my immense relief he did get back safely.

CHAPTER XXIV

The Battle of the Crossing of the Rhine

Early in the spring of 1945, Tac Army left their winter quarters in buildings and resumed the camping out that was appropriate to mobile warfare. But Ian MacNaughton, the Squadron Captain, had a genius for ensuring that no man was ever more uncomfortable than necessary and in this I agreed with him. So one day I was not really surprised to learn that our entire SHQ were to be billeted in a convent for two nights. 'Sister Cook' was an absolute genius and her gigantic trifle ornamented by the Second Army Shield on top was something to be remembered. There was a piano in the Convent, and our brilliant airman pianist organized a concert and sing-song for all ranks.

The Crossing of the Rhine was for us the last great set battle of the War. We heard that Winston Churchill was coming out to watch it and we half expected an order to take him up and give him a proper view. But no such order came. Incidentally one of my former pupils at Larkhill, Vic Cowley, had flown HM The King in Italy.

On the 20th of March 1945, I did four photo runs down the Rhine. On three of them I was accompanied by Cpl Wadhams and on the fourth by Cpl Hazelden. I did two more the following day. They were done at heights varying from 1,000 to 2,300 feet and I kept at it until I was satisfied with the results.

The first difficulty was that a formidable smokescreen had been put down on our side of the Rhine. This was presumably intended to prevent the enemy seeing what we were doing. David Cover of 'B' Flight subsequently wrote that they had had the doubtful pleasure of living in Montgomery's smokescreen for ten days and that it had given them excellent practice in blind approach landings but had put them off their compo rations.

The other difficulty for us was that enemy 88 mm and 20 mm guns would persist in shooting at us and I wondered whether this was because they had not been in Normandy and so had never been taught by us not to do so. A more likely explanation was that by reason of the smoke they realized that it was really impracticable for us to retaliate.

Opposing the British 21st Army Group were several excellent German parachute divisions and the remaining German armour. It was therefore not going to be an easy battle to fight. During the night of the 23rd/24th March our massed artillery kept up a continuous and devastating fire at the enemy across the Rhine while the 51st Highland Division, the 1st Commando Brigade and the 15th Scottish Division each established bridgeheads across the river under cover of darkness, being ferried across by 'Buffaloes' (ie armoured amphibious craft each of which carried about twenty-eight men). I believe the Black Watch were the first across the Rhine in the British Sector. An anticipated immediate counter-attack by the German armour would have to come either through Rees or through Wesel. So the objective given to the 51st Highland Division was the town of Rees and the 1st Commando Brigade's objective was Wesel. Their orders were to capture and hold these objectives until the arrival of the Airborne Troops the following morning. They succeeded in this brilliantly. The artillery fire and a heavy raid by RAF bombers on Wesel during that night and the darkness

During the Battle of the Crossing of the Rhine I found myself surrounded by the gliders and had no alternative but to go with them.

Gliders on the ground.

Parachutes stuck in trees.

Wesel after its devastation during the night of 23/24th of March 1945.

made it very difficult for the enemy to carry out immediate counter-attacks or to find out precisely what was going on. The artillery fire was timed to cease abruptly at 0950 hrs when the airborne troops were to arrive.

We had been ordered not to fly until the bombardment had ceased as no guns were available for random tasks. We were also warned that our artillery were using for the first time 'proximity fuses' which would detonate if they were to pass anywhere near an aircraft.

Immediately the bombardment ceased, several squadrons of large four-engined bombers flying very low passed over us and dropped our paratroops the other side of the Rhine. These aircraft were so low that I wondered how the parachutes could possibly open in time. The enemy flak had obviously not been neutralized by the bombardment and our aircraft were to sustain very heavy casualties, particularly as they were turning for home after dropping the paratroops.

I took off so as to be able to watch what was going on. This was most unwise as I soon found myself surrounded by an apparently endless stream of our aircraft which were towing gliders, and, as I was unwilling to risk a collision by turning, I had to go with them until I had climbed above them. Across the Rhine all hell had been let loose and the sky was filled by flak and machine-gun tracer. After what seemed an age I was glad to get back safely to my ALG.

When I landed I found that an American glider had come down on our side of the Rhine and not far from our ALG, and the troops had all come running out of it ready to do battle, only to find that they were amongst friends who were delighted to welcome them to lunch.

That day and the following day I flew six sorties. Our troops were being ferried across the Rhine in Buffaloes and launches and the sappers were building bridges of boats with amazing speed so as to get our tanks across. Our front line on the other side of the river was very nebulous and I could do no more than watch, photograph and report what I had seen.

By the morning of the 26th of March the time had come for me to find a suitable Tac Army HQ for the Army Commander the other side of the Rhine. He habitually chose, if possible, to site his caravan in the park of some mansion or castle – he never entered the building. And our ALG had to be within a short walk of his caravan. I studied the map and found an obvious site, Schloss Diersfordt. It was about a mile beyond the river and on the border between our sector and the American sector.

I took an airman, LAC Clutterbrook, with me and I told him to bring a rifle as we might meet some of the enemy. I had only my revolver. The castle was old and imposing. It was surrounded on three sides by a moat full of water and on one side, outside the moat, was a finely constructed garden. One side of the courtyard was a building which had probably housed carriages in days gone by. Now it had been filled with cattle and it had been destroyed during the bombardment. It was still burning, the cattle were all dead and the stench a few days later would be appalling.

The other side of a small orchard was a field which I selected for a landing strip. It was pockmarked with shell holes and littered with discarded parachutes and unburied dead. Fortunately, no gliders had landed in this field: they usually landed in close groups in order to come out fighting near each other.

With great care I selected a landing path and after doing a dummy run in order to inspect these hazards more closely, I came in between two trees and landed successfully without hitting any obstruction or coming to grief in a shell hole. Obviously much work would need to be done before that field could be used as the Army Commander's ALG. As I landed I was fully aware that if I 'pranged' the aircraft it might be days before we could get back across the Rhine.

I taxied up to the corner of the field nearest the castle, where there was a gap in the hedge leading to a path across the orchard and there I switched off.

Clutterbrook and I took the path across the orchard, round a clump of trees and then to the bridge which crossed the moat. On the way we passed a burnt-out German armoured vehicle and a few German dead by it amongst whom I saw a soldier who could not have been more than fifteen years of age. On the bridge was an American soldier who was shooting with his rifle the ornamental ducks on the moat. I wondered what he was supposed to be doing there: ducks at that time of year would not be worth eating.

Opposite the entrance to the castle was a building in which we saw a Mercedes-Benz. It was jacked up on wooden blocks and there was no sign of its wheels. We were short of transport and such a splendid car would be very useful to us. So I told Clutterbrook to look for the wheels and to try to get the car into working order. I then went up a stately flight of stone steps to the front door of the castle.

The front door had been broken open and the front hall and the passageway beyond were in a state of absolute chaos. There was a gigantic safe which someone had apparently tried to open with explosives. But the safe had won.

From the passage a flight of stone steps led down to the cellars. It was such a castle as might even have dungeons down below. I guessed that the castle's occupants were probably all in the cellars. There were several reception rooms which had been sacked as if by burglars looking for any small objects of value or usefulness. One can scarcely blame a victorious army for doing a bit of looting in the country of their enemies, but it is sad to witness the result. There were no pictures: they had probably been taken down and stored in the cellars or dungeons. For all I knew, there might be German soldiers hiding in the cellars but I did not intend to investigate.

In one reception room, which had a door at each end, there was a Steinway grand piano the lid of which had been badly damaged by some burning object, but the burn had not quite got through to the mechanism. It was a fairly new Steinway and to my surprise it was in perfect working order and in tune. So I sat down and began to play.

My thoughts were confused as I played Chopin's 'Berceuse'. I felt a deep sense of shame at being in some way connected with the destruction of this lovely home. I told myself that Hitler's countrymen had fully deserved all this, but I could not bring myself to believe such a thing. Before the War, I had liked and admired many Germans and I had loved one German girl. In any event the spectacle of human and animal suffering had always appalled me.

As the 'Berceuse' came to an end, enemy shells began to fall nearby and it occurred to me that the castle might be their target. The Germans might expect us to use this building as a Headquarters, though in fact British troops very rarely occupied any building during a battle. Foxholes were far safer. I was not ready to go: that piano was a joy not to be missed. I began to play Chopin's 'Revolutionary Study' – very badly but well enough to express my feelings at that time.

A shell crashed into the East Wing of the castle and the whole room shook. But the ceiling held. An old man, whom I took to be a family retainer, passed through the room and went out by another door carrying a bucket of water. He did this several times and I assumed that he was trying to put out a fire caused by that shell. We ignored each other.

Another shell crashed near the castle. It appeared to be only harrassing fire, but I did not want my aircraft damaged. I decided to play the 'Liebesträume' and then go. As I reached the first cadenza I sensed that I was no longer alone.

A slim and lovely girl with golden hair was standing in an open doorway. She was silent

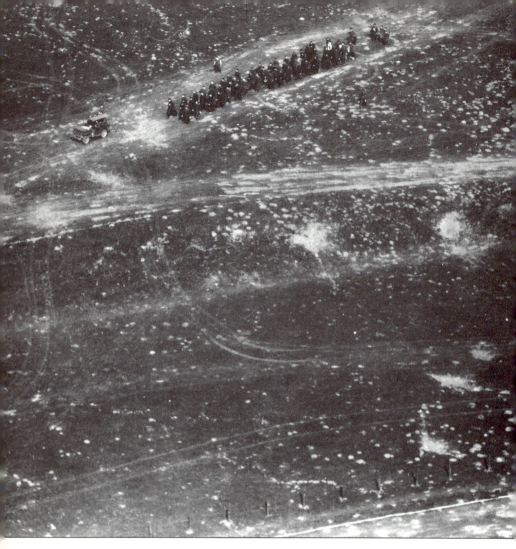

Photo taken across the Rhine at 1400 hrs on the 24th of March 1945 of German POWs being marched back to the Rhine. I wondered how they would get them across.

The 51st Highland Division beginning to arrive on the far bank of the Rhine.

The Field Dressing Station across the Rhine.

The progress of the first bridge across the Rhine at 1630 hrs on the 25th of March 1945.

Our Tac Army ALG at Schloss Diersfordt.

Schloss Diersfordt as it was before it was destroyed.

and quite motionless. Her face was very white and her eyes reflected sadness and despair. She was wearing a dark blue skiing outfit which was probably the best thing for living in cellars. She must have come up to see who was playing her piano. Perhaps the music had transformed me into a kind and courteous human being: at any rate I felt ashamed.

I think I have said enough. I have told this sad story because it gives some colour to the views which I am going to set down in my next chapter.

The following day I moved my SHQ to the Diersfordt field: we had much to do clearing it up. As I arrived there by air I saw that the castle had become overnight a more or less complete ruin. I did not go near it again. The Army Commander moved his caravan into the orchard. A day or two later the tide of battle moved on and we moved with it.

On the 30th of March, I was asked by Brigadier Campbell, the Chief Engineer, to photograph the Rhine bridges. I took this opportunity to take a few photographs of Diersfordt as it held memories for me. Incidentally Clutterbrook had not found the wheels of that Mercedes-Benz and I was glad of this.

CHAPTER XXV

The Order Against Fraternisation

When we had first crossed the German border after the battle of the Siegfried Line, I visited each Flight in turn and talked to all ranks about the orders which had reached us forbidding fraternisation with any Germans. I understood that these orders had been originated by the politicians.

I did not go so far as to preach the then popular theme that the only good German was a dead German. But I said that it was obviously unthinkable that any of us should be on terms of friendship with people when we were under a duty to fight against their relations, friends and fellow countrymen.

So we were not to shake hands with our enemies, we were not even to speak to German girls however beautiful or inviting they might be and we were not to lodge in any German house unless we had first turned all its German occupants out of it. To disobey this order would be a court martial offence.

I could see some slight sense in this order, but I did resent being ordered to be a thoroughly unpleasant person. It appeared to be based on the assumption that all Germans were to be blamed by us for the evils committed by Hitler and his thugs. Now, forty years later, I am inclined to link the non-fraternisation order with the absurd requirement of unconditional surrender: they went together.

Yalta was a diplomatic triumph for Stalin. He realized that the German Army would welcome a peace with us whereby the Allies would occupy all Germany. We only learned at the very end of the War of the agreement made by Stalin, Roosevelt and Churchill at Yalta when our forward troops, who were on their way to Berlin, were ordered back to the line which had been agreed at that conference.

Surely our Allied politicians should have announced as soon as we had landed in Normandy that our aim was to liberate Germany from Hitler, his thugs and the SS and restore democratic government. And we should have extended the hand of friendship to all other Germans including the German Army. If we had done that, the War would surely have been over by July 1944.

When we eventually entered Germany we found that many large cities had been razed to the ground and Hamburg was a terrible sight of complete devastation. But the Germans fought on. They could not accept that word 'unconditional', and it in effect united them behind Hitler.

After the War there was some criticism of 'Bomber' Harris for having caused this devastation. This was quite unfair both to him and to all the magnificent young men who flew the bombers and gave their lives in the cause of freedom. They had taught the German people the folly of continuing the War, but their success was nullified by our Allied politicians who prevented the German Army from giving up the struggle.

Not long ago I read the autobiography of Princess Tatiana von Metternich who was born a

Russian princess and married an Austrian prince of illustrious family. She strongly criticised the Allies for failing to recognize the distinction between the evil Nazi leaders and their SS supporters on the one hand and the good mass of the German people on the other. She drew a similar distinction between the Russian Comintern and KGB on the one hand and the good mass of the Russian people on the other. Stalin murdered 6,000,000 of his political opponents whereas Hitler murdered 4,000,000 of his. The good mass of the German people after their eventual liberation resented being referred to, particularly by the American officers, as 'bloody Nazis'.

A few years ago I had a long conversation on a train journey with a former German Jew who had escaped from the Nazis shortly before the War. He liked and admired the good mass of the German people and would not say anything against them. He predicted that we in Britain would have, sooner or later, a Marxist dictatorship similar to those of Hitler and Stalin. A democracy is by its very nature quite unable to protect itself from persistent evil propaganda which preaches hate and turns truth upside-down. In Russia the hate was directed towards the capitalists: in Germany the Jews were blamed for everything that went wrong as a result of the errors of the government.

Just imagine what would happen in Britain if a Marxist government with a programme of CND and unilateral disarmament were ever to get into power here. Parliament would be abolished and replaced by a self-perpetuating comintern. The armed forces would be dispensed with, as we could never defend ourselves against any country which had a single atomic bomb with which to threaten us. Every possible political opponent of the Marxist government would be liquidated, as in Russia and Germany, by thugs in concentration camps. Most Russian nuclear missile sites threatening America would be moved to the west coast of Britain in the mistaken belief that America might possibly hesitate to destroy Britain in order to save themselves.

All this is so obvious (except to certain bishops and so-called 'peace women') that I have only mentioned it as it provides food for thought as to whether the good mass of the German people should have been so unjustly blamed for the evils done by Hitler.

Now I must get back to my Memoirs of long ago. But before doing so I will say that, provided our electorate never swallow the propaganda of the CND movement, there will never be another major war. Wars are only started by political leaders who believe that they are certain to win and that they will derive great advantage from winning. No fool on Earth is going to start a nuclear war which would inevitably result in his being either killed in the war or torn to pieces by the infuriated populace. This is quite obvious.

CHAPTER XXVI
Belsen Concentration Camp

Shortly after we had crossed the Rhine, we heard that the Army Commander had somehow received a message from the enemy advising him to avoid sending any troops to Belsen because, it was said, there was an outbreak of some form of plague there. In fact he sent tanks there with all possible speed and as soon as Belsen had been liberated, Moke Murray flew the Brigadier in charge of the Army Medical Service to the camp.

Moke went into the camp with the Brigadier, and they were shown round by the Camp Commandant, who was later known as the 'Beast of Belsen'. Moke told me afterwards that the Camp Commandant insisted that he had merely been obeying orders and seemed quite unable to understand that he had been doing anything wrong. This attitude so irritated the Brigadier that finally he was provoked into saying to the Camp Commandant, 'Surely you know that you will be hanged for this.' As the SS guards had not yet been disarmed Moke thought this remark a little tactless.

The Camp Commandant protested strenuously at the disarming of his SS guards. He said that the prisoners were like wild animals and would tear the SS guards to pieces as soon as these were no longer able to defend themselves. This did not in fact happen, as British soldiers took over and put the SS guards to work clearing up the mess. Shortly afterwards I flew low round Belsen and took photographs. Bulldozers were being used to inter the vast heaps of unburied dead who all appeared to be little more than skin and bone. It was a dreadful sight.

I think that Brigadier did a magnificent job. He immediately established a 'human laundry' wherein every prisoner was first completely shaved of all hair and then scrubbed with a liquid solution of DDT in order to kill lice. We heard no more talk of plague and I think many of the prisoners recovered from the physical effects of their terrible ordeal. Incidentally it was later learned that when starving men are beginning to recover their strength they are filled with very strong sexual desires. I don't know about starving women.

CHAPTER XXVII
The Final Stages of the War

When we had chased a defeated German Army from Normandy to Brussels we thought that the War was virtually over and that we would soon be in Berlin. We thought this again once our Allied Armies had crossed the Rhine. Surely the Germans would surrender rather than have their own country further devastated. But they fought on.

Princess Tatiana also criticised us for having advanced so slowly after we had crossed the Rhine. She said that as a result of this the good Germans had to wait so long before they were liberated from the murdering SS troops. Since the unsuccessful coup in July 1944, thousands of good Germans had been executed merely on suspicion. But one must not be surprised if our soldiers were unwilling to take unnecessary risks when the end of the War was obviously so near. The Germans were fighting desperately and heroically for, and in, their own country – as we would have fought if Britain had been invaded in 1940.

Every river crossing was stoutly defended. They brought out everything they had left to fight with. Peter Kroyer took on and destroyed an armoured train which was something the Air OP had never seen before. Every village was barricaded, presumably by the 'were-wolves', but our tanks went straight through and woe betide any village that had not put out white flags before the tanks arrived. The tanks were preceded by our Austers so that we might report on white flags and any likely resistance which might lie ahead. It was on this task that Mackie of 'C' Flight had his self-sealing petrol tank holed by a German rifle bullet, but he got down safely without sustaining any further damage. The petrol tank was soon replaced.

On the rare occasions on which I went anywhere by road, I saw crowds of weeping women beside the road watching us go through. I felt sorrow rather than any sense of triumphal progress.

We saw for the first time the new German jet aircraft which flew so fast that it did not worry us in the least.

On the 4th of May, the day before hostilities with Germany ceased, I received an order to send a pilot with aircraft to 21 Army Group – ie Montgomery's HQ. I sent Ian Young. Shortly afterwards Ian got me on th R/T and said that another aircraft was needed and I replied that I would fly over immediately and join him. The terms of surrender had been signed at Lüneburg and we were to fly the two top German generals to Kiel immediately so that they could give the necessary orders that all hostilities were to cease at 0800 hrs the following morning.

It was clear to us that this was a suicide job both for us and the generals. Fighting was still going on, and we would have to fly over the German Army who would have no reason not to shoot us down. Even if we were to surmount this obstacle, Kiel was a German naval port and so it and its airfield would be heavily defended by anti-aircraft guns. Ground vehicles might carry white flags which would give them some protection but there was no equivalent for aircraft. However, we were not going to argue with the Commander-in-Chief about his orders. If we were at tree-top height we might get through.

Fortunately for us the German generals did not share our scruples concerning arguing with Montgomery. At the last moment they flatly refused to go by air. So Montgomery had no alternative but to send them by road. One of his staff who went with the generals was killed on the journey. Incidentally the C-in-C lost an ADC not many days later as a result of a visit to a Russian HQ. This ADC had far too many vodkas, became completely drunk and started firing his revolver in his enthusiasm. As the C-in-C was himself a strict teetotaller, this ADC was lucky to be merely dismissed for the offence.

A few days before hostilities ended, a German Army Commander arrived in his staff car at our Tac Army. He asked Dempsey to accept the surrender of his entire Army. The Commander asked the German General where his Army was, and, on being told that it was facing the Russian advance, he refused this request. The German Army Commander thereupon left, but returned shortly afterwards and insisted on surrendering himself. This the Commander could not refuse to accept, but he did indicate that he despised an Army Commander who deserted his Army.

On the day when hostilities ceased, 'B' Flight moved to Kiel Aerodrome. That day and the following day a succession of German fighter pilots landed there, anxious to surrender to us rather than to the Russians. One of these overshot the airfield and crashed his aircraft: Peter Kroyer (who spoke fluent German) told him what a bloody awful landing he had done. The German pilot smiled and said, 'I didn't think I would be needing the aircraft again.'

I have referred to the 'werewolves' and perhaps I should say more about them. During the fighting in Germany, Hitler ordered all German civilians to become werewolves, behaving like harmless civilians by day and becoming commando soldiers by night or whenever opportunity offered. One could pass through an apparently harmless village every house of which had put out a white flag and yet be fired at by a rifle at unexpected times when in solitary places.

There was an occasion when Ian MacNaughton and I were in a clearing in a wood while we were looking for a suitable ALG. Someone started shooting at us with a rifle. We lost no time in getting back into the jeep and hurrying away. Ian accelerated to a perilous speed along the bumpy track. One bullet passed just above the top of my head but I was much more worried by the risk of being bumped out of the jeep than by any bullets.

One evening a 'Queen Mary' with its airman driver and a corporal of the RAF Regiment arrived at our ALG. They had been sent to fetch an RAF aircraft which had crash landed near the front line and they had come to seek our company and protection during that night. They were certainly wise not to park for the night beside a road in hostile country. We had been lent an armoured car as a result of the risk of any solitary vehicle being attacked.

That night some werewolves attacked. The first we knew of it was when a bomb was thrown into a tent of a commando unit that was camped nearby and some commandos were killed. After that we all stood to and there was a great deal of shooting, but none of us were hurt. That corporal of the RAF Regiment appeared to enjoy himself immensely: at last he was seeing some fighting.

I have wondered whether the whole idea of the RAF Regiment was not a mistake. Many excellent chaps were trained for war and yet never saw any fighting. On the other hand many of our infantry saw far too much fighting and they would have been glad of an occasional rest guarding aerodromes.

I think these werewolves were mostly 'Hitler Youth' who had been completely indoctin-

All ranks of SHQ at Hartfield, May 1944.

Left to right, 4th row, back: Smith, Tyson, ——, Newall, Herbert, ——, ——, Chatburn, ——, ——, Warde, Smith, Turner. 3rd row: ——, Osborne, Wigley, Weeks, Graham, Williams, Ethel, ——, 'Doc', Lindsay, Flemming, Clarke, ——, ——, Ferguson, Taylor. 2nd row: Clutterbrook, Griffiths, Vowles, ——, Banks, Oliver, Barratt, Sergeant Harris, Smith, Bombardier Hicks, Davies, Woodhouse, Dunderdale, ——, Mansfield, Wadhams. Front row: Sergeants Hathaway, Darke, Flemming, Warrant Officer Easton, Lieutenant Barry, Flight Lieutenant Foley, Flight Lieutenant MacQueen (the Adj), Captain McNaughton, the Author, Captains Kroyer and Montagu, Lieutenant Harding, Captain Murphy, Evans, Harrison, Sergeant Budden.

All ranks of 'A' Flight at Lüneberg, May 1945.

Left to right, seated: RAF Corporal Fitter ——, ——, Laurie Denton, Denis Wright, Jimmy Storie, Tom Topping, Jimmy MacLean, ——, ——.

All ranks of 'B' Flight at Lüneberg, May 1945.

Left to right, seated: LAC ———, the RAF Flight Corporal Fitter ———, Peter Kroyer, Eric Levison, David Cover, John Phillips, Charles Keen, Sergeant Daglish, Bombardier Harrison.

All ranks of 'C' Flight at Hartfield, May 1944.

Those seated, from left to right, are: Bombardier Jones (Flight Wireless Operator and Clerk), Jimmy Magrath, James Stunt, Paul Gillespie, Moke Murray, Harry Salter, Roy Hill, Sergeant Matthews (the Army Sergeant in charge of 'C' Flight and an excellent man for the job. He had won the Military Medal in North Africa for shooting down a low-flying Messerschmidt with a Boyes anti-tank rifle fired from the hip – a unique achievement. He had a great sense of humour and was always cheerful), Corporal Thompson (the RAF Corporal Fitter, a red-haired marine engineer from the Clyde). The rather blurred dog in the foreground was 'Nigger', the Flight mascot. He was acquired somewhere in England some months before D-Day and mysteriously spirited across to Normandy where, to the great sorrow of everyone, he eventually deserted us in favour of a French girl friend. In those days stray dogs frequently attached themselves to Army cookhouses. He was probably visiting a bitch in season when 'C' Flight moved to a new ALG.

The officers of 658 AOP Squadron after the cessation of hostilities, Lüneburg, May 1945.

Left to right, standing: Charles Keen, Geoffrey Waters, Eric Levison, Paul Gillespie, Peter Kroyer, Jimmy Maclean, Ian Young, John Phillips, Harry Salter, James Stunt, Allan Mackie, Oliver Murphy, David Cover. Seated: Richard McQueen (the Adj), Ian McNaughton, Tom Topping, Monty, Moke Murray, the Author, Tony Knight, Jimmy Storie, Laurie Denton, Norman Foley.

ated with the Nazi view that they must fight on until the end. The German Army had had enough: so had we all. Most Germans would have been friendly towards us if we had been permitted to fraternise with them. One day two of our trucks were bogged down in a field and we could not get them out. So I sent Peter Kroyer to the nearest farm to borrow a couple of cart horses. The farmer came immediately with two fine horses and they quickly pulled the trucks on to firm ground.

After the end of hostilities one of our divisional commanders paid a courtesy visit to the Russian general whose division was facing him across the River Elbe. The Russian chose to entertain him by taking him to watch Russian soldiers shooting German soldiers and civilians who were trying to swim across the Elbe to our side of the river. It was a sickening sight.

We had captured a Fieseler Storch, and once hostilities were ended this became the Commander's aircraft. We painted the Second Army shield on it. It was a fantastic aircraft for taking off and for landing in only a few yards, even better than the Vigilant. After the oil pressure had fallen to a dangerously low level when I was taking a Tac Army officer to have a look at Hamburg, we gave it a very thorough overhaul before handing it over to Oliver for use by the Commander.

On VE-Day (Victory in Europe), there was a tremendous party at Tac Army. We had a large bonfire and we fired off our entire supply of Very cartridges in lieu of fireworks. The following day Peter Kroyer flew over to one of the Danish islands (without any order to do so) and said that he had come to accept the formal surrender of the German troops stationed there. He then proceeded to confiscate all or part of their alcoholic drinks. He returned to us with twelve cases of champagne and twelve cases of brandy. I could not protest because I shared the loot. In any event, on my way back from a photo run of the Elbe bridges which I had done for Brigadier Campbell, I had landed on another Danish island. In my case there were no German troops, but I was welcomed by the Danish inhabitants.

I personally never flew any passenger into the Russian Zone, but several of my pilots did this and found the Russians very friendly. But a month or so later they ceased to fraternise with us and we believed that this was in consequence of orders which they had received from Moscow.

One day several of us flew to a town just south of the Danish border. We watched German soldiers marching out of Denmark. One of us got hold of Goering's armoured Mercedes-Benz. It was a colossal and very luxurious bullet-proof car. We decided to find out how fast it would go on the runway of Schleswig Airfield. We got it up to 100 mph but nearly crashed it when trying to stop before the runway ended. It was too heavy for its brakes.

One day I saw a vast crowd of German prisoners-of-war. They had been herded on an airfield and I learned subsequently that there were 57,000 of them. There was a British soup kitchen which had to cope with them somehow. I landed to investigate. Someone offered me a gold sovereign for twenty cigarettes. I was not in the business of selling cigarettes and so gave away all I had with me.

Then a German fighter pilot came to talk to me. He was a charming man and he reminded me of my German friends of before the War. There was so much for us to talk about. He asked me to let him take up my Auster for a circuit. I was not that stupid: he might have flown to his home in it and that would have required a lot of explaining by me.

General Dempsey was one of the finest men that I have ever known. He had a brilliant brain which went straight to the heart of any matter and his judgment was always sound. I never saw him annoyed, agitated or angry. He was calm, courteous and kind. I am not

'B' Flight accepting the surrender of the Luftwaffe at Kiel. Note the four tiny Austers.

Tac Army ALG at Lüneberg.

Above: Sam Maidment (my driver/batman who had followed me from the Dorset Yeomanry) standing by my staff car with Ian McNaughton the Squadron Captain.

Tom Topping, left and Ian McNaughton, right.

Captain 'Dickie' Dawson (left) briefing
General Sir Miles Dempsey as to the map
references of the various HQs to which the
General was to fly that day. Photograph
taken at Tac Army ALG at Lille St Hubert
in December of 1944, probably by Oliver
Murphy who was waiting nearby with his
aircraft ready to take off with the General.

Murray Bell. In March 1945 he
handed over command of 'A'
Flight to Jimmy Storie and took
over command of 662 Squadron
from Alec Hill.

Left to right: Moke Murray, Harry Salter, Mevrouw Van Keulen, James Stunt and Paul Gillespie. Moke and his 'C' Flight had, at that time, an ALG at Helmond, and the officers were billeted in the lovely home of the Van Keulens. Moke says of Mevrouw Van Keulen: 'She was marvellous and mothered us all, so we called her "Mooder" just like her other five children. The Van Keulens came over to England after the war and I went back and stayed with them for a week in 1948.'

suggesting that he did not sack any general or brigadier under him whom he thought inadequate. It was his job to have the best people under him. And he preferred to have under him officers who had served him well in the past and whom he had learned to trust. He was like Montgomery in this respect. It might be argued that General Bucknill was unfairly sacked in Normandy when he was replaced by General Horrocks, who had served under Montgomery in North Africa and had been severely wounded there. But Horrocks proved to be such an outstanding general and so popular with those under him that surely the sacking of Bucknill was entirely justified.

But I am not qualified to express any opinion as to the abilities of generals. I will just say that I, and all of us at Tac Army, were devoted to General Dempsey, and thought far more of him than of Montgomery. Dempsey got on very well with all the American generals, whereas Montgomery was tactless and much too inclined to annoy them by his assumption that he was the greatest of them all.

HM The King came out to Germany and lunched at Tac Army. I was of course not there, but we heard from the ADCs what had happened. Montgomery dominated the conversation. He said, 'Soon I think I will retire and perhaps become a bishop. Whenever I think it necessary I will make a pronouncement', etc. Later he said to the King, 'Winston is too old:

General Dempsey and Oliver Murphy standing in front of the General's Auster.

he ought to retire.' There was an instant hush as everyone there, except Montgomery, knew that this remark should not have been publicly made, even by a Field Marshal, to the King about his Prime Minister. Then the King smiled and said, 'Well, Field Marshal, you have just made your first pronouncement.'

I later heard a story that Winston Churchill had said to the King, 'I think Montgomery wants my job', and the King had replied, 'I thought it was my job that he was after.'

CHAPTER XXVIII

Captain Claud Cecil Ballyn, DFC and Bar, RA

After the War I wrote the following obituary:

On the 1st of October 1942, Ballyn (always known as 'Charles') began his flying training at No1 EFTS. He was then 36 years of age and, judged by Air OP standards, an old man. Men over 30 are apt to experience very considerable difficulty in acquiring the knack of low flying and short landings, but they normally have the compensating advantages of being reliable and of never taking any unnecessary risks. Charles had the lack of ability consistent with his years and yet the recklessness of youth, and this combination proved alarming to his instructors and dangerous to himself.

On the 14th of October, on his second solo flight, he stalled when coming in to land and had his first accident. Very little was left of the Tiger Moth and Charles went to hospital with cuts on his face, injuries to his back, both ankles broken and one leg seriously injured. A less determined pilot would never have flown again, but Charles continued his flying training seven weeks later.

His career at 43 OTU was far from being distinguished. He was a very slow learner and had a minor accident which very nearly resulted in his being suspended from flying. After leaving the OTU he joined 658 Air OP Squadron, and a month later destroyed another aircraft. When taking part in a Flight exercise, he flew over his ground party at an RV at about 15 feet above the ground and at 60 mph and attempted to drop a message. The message bag became entangled in the port wing strut and Charles promptly attempted to disengage it without first ensuring that he had plenty of throttle and height – with the result that he flew into the ground. For this incident he received a red endorsement in his log book and a warning that if there should be any repetition of this unfortunate episode he would be returned to regimental duty. But we all liked him and greatly admired his tenacity, and in fact he was given several more chances.

About a fortnight later, I set 'B' Flight a 48-hour exercise and on the evening of the second day we reached an ALG about five miles south of Newbury. The pilots had by then all done a considerable amount of night flying, and the exercise was to end with a dusk flight back to Old Sarum. I pointed out to the three other pilots that all they had to do was fly on a course until they reached the railway line running from Andover to Salisbury and then follow it home. At 2200 hrs we took off individually in perfect weather at intervals of about two minutes.

I took off last, flew into a storm with low cloud and torrential rain, but arrived safely at Old Sarum where I found to my horror that none of the other three had arrived. The next hour was one of the worst that I ever remember. We illuminated the flarepath and waited in the Watch Office. Then Charles McCorry rang up from Thruxton and said that as he had flown over the aerodrome there the duty pilot had very obligingly lit the flarepath for him and so, owing to the storm, he had landed.

Then Tony Knight, the Flight Commander, rang up and said he had landed in a field near Winchester. He had decided to follow Charles Ballyn and keep an eye on him and Charles had, of course, followed the wrong railway line. Tony, realizing that there was no time to be wasted, had opened to full throttle and endeavoured to catch him up and then lead him home. But Charles was also flying at full throttle and was quite impossible to catch and so Tony wisely chose a field and landed in it before it was quite dark.

And Charles flew on through the night and the storm. Eventually the telephone in the Watch Office at Old Sarum rang once again – Charles had landed intact in a field beside the flashing beacon at Lopcombe Corner. I was far too relieved to be angry with him.

During the ensuing ten months, Charles' flying improved very considerably and he began to acquire a reputation for being an expert shot, though he did have a much criticised tendency to fly too far forward. But it was only after he landed in Normandy with 'B' Flight on the 18th of June 1944 that Charles really began to be appreciated and an asset to the Air OP.

In operations no one minded how far forward he flew so long as he achieved the right results without being shot down. In bad visibility and in the smoke and dust of battle we all had to be prepared to fly over the front line. It was only natural that Charles should have been one of the first to demonstrate that this could be done.

In conditions of low cloud when wiser pilots remained on the ground, he was always ready and keen to try, by the most unorthodox methods, to carry out any tasks which he had been given – such as searching for enemy tanks or, by his mere presence, discouraging enemy mortars from firing for fear that they might be located. On one such occasion when he was on a reconnaissance of the FDLs at Ondefontaine in Normandy, he spotted a number of enemy infantry in an orchard not very far from some of our own tanks. So he promptly landed beside the tanks, climbed into one of them and went 'Boche hunting' with them. His excuse afterwards was that the cloud had come down so low that he had doubted that he would be able to fly back to his ALG, and so he had decided to occupy his time profitably while waiting for the cloud to lift. Five hours later he returned to his aircraft and flew back to his ALG where, being very tired, he misjudged his landing and ran off the narrow strip on to some soft ground, which caused the aircraft to turn upside-down.

On the 4th of September 1944, he, with the rest of 'B' Flight, landed at Brussels Airport – among the first British aircraft to land there since the occupation. It was a memorable and triumphant occasion, as they were mobbed by an excited crowd and at the same time shelled by a German 88 mm battery from close range. However, no damage was done and the following day Charles was entrusted with the task of flying General Horrocks from Brussels to Tactical Army Headquarters at Blairville. The choice of pilot was unfortunate as Charles was so overcome by the honour and responsibility that he got lost on the way and had to land in a field and ask where he was. But the General took it very well indeed and not merely forgave his pilot but expressly asked to be flown by the same pilot on the following day. Fortunately this lapse was never repeated.

From that time onwards Charles never 'put up another black'. He did magnificent work both by day and by moonlight. His Flight went with 5 AGRA to Nijmegen, then to Armstenrade, then to the extremely difficult ALGs amid the snow of the Ardennes and then back to the Reichswald for the final assault on the Siegfried Line. And he never damaged another aircraft. On one occasion in November 1944 it was essential to find out whether the enemy were occupying a certain trench system south-west of Arnhem. The clouds were low and it was a day on which it was just possible to fly but quite impossible to observe, so that there was only one way of finding the answer to this question. Charles flew low straight to the trench system, which he found to be occupied, and he was heavily engaged by the enemy's defences. For this he was awarded his first DFC.

His last flight was his greatest flight of all. It was on the 19th of February 1945 and he had been detailed to observe an enemy battery area, fire from which was holding up our advance towards Keppeln. In poor visibility and in spite of low clouds, he flew close to the enemy position where he was engaged by small arms fire. He received a mortal wound from a bullet which passed through his back and lodged in his abdomen. In spite of his great pain, he flew back to a difficult ALG on which he had never landed before, carried out a dummy run, made a perfect landing, taxied clear of the strip and switched off. He then collapsed.

From this wound Charles died, but the memory of his fearless spirit lived on and inspired the pilots of 'B' Flight through their ordeal during the Battle of the Rhine Crossing. The massed guns were firing continuously and it appeared sheer suicide to fly for long periods in front of them. But 51st Highland Division were suffering heavy casualties from many batteries of enemy SP guns, which the Flight was called upon to locate and neutralize. And in the smoke of the battle the only way to locate these batteries was to fly over them – in the path of our own shells. This all the pilots of the Flight did unhesitatingly; nor did the remaining three, Tony Knight, David Cover and Peter Kroyer, flinch even after Terry Wykes and his observer LAC McNairney had been hit by a shell and crashed to their deaths behind the enemy lines.

During his Air OP career, Charles consistently broke all the rules except one – the infantry, whom we admired so much, must be supported, whatever the risk. Perhaps this was the only rule that really mattered: certainly there are many infantrymen alive today who have cause to remember him with grateful hearts.

CHAPTER XXIX
Epilogue

At the end of June 1945, Dempsey gave up his command in Germany and went to Oxford to supervise the writing of the official history of the France / Germany Campaign. He asked me to form a special flight from my Squadron which would go back to England with him as his personal Flight. Though his place of work was to be at Oxford, he himself and his ADC (Henry Whitworth) were to live in a country house near Chipping Norton. I chose a few very special RAF fitters and riggers and Army drivers for this Flight: Corporal Eric Oliver (who was an expert at absolutely everything including cutting our General's hair), Corporal Griffiths (who had been Oliver Murphy's observer in Normandy), LAC Taylor, LAC Wise, and Gunners Weeks and Williams. Ian Young and I each took an Auster and Oliver Murphy took the Commander's Fieseler Storch. We adopted Chipping Norton as our airfield.

It was a sad day for me when my whole Squadron were paraded for me to say goodbye to them. We had been through a great deal together and I had grown very fond of them all. They were a superb body of men and I regarded them as personal friends.

General Dempsey's wishes were for me a magic wand with which I could organize every posting which I desired with either the Army or the RAF Record Office, Gloucester. In July, Diana joined me in Chipping Norton and later we rented a house by the river in Oxford and this was our very first home together after our marriage in February 1943.

Those were golden days. Oliver flew the General in the Fieseler Storch and I flew Henry in an Auster to Royal Ascot. The General was in the Royal Box with the King and Queen and Henry, Oliver and I were guests of the Airborne people. To land beside the Course was the way to arrive at Ascot and it was a most enjoyable day.

We flew the General and Henry wherever they wanted to go. Then Dempsey was given command of the 14th Army in the Far East which was to finish off the war against Japan. But, once the nuclear bombs had been dropped, there was little more to do there except sort things out.

On the 18th of August 1945, Oliver and I flew the General and Henry to Hurn whence they were to go by a York to the Far East. Oliver went with the General as pilot-cum-ADC.

Dempsey asked me to try to hang on to the Fieseler Storch for him so that he would be able to have it again when he returned to Europe. So Ian Young and I flew to Rearsby with the Fieseler Storch, and persuaded our good friends there to hide it and to look after it for Dempsey.

Hiding it from the Air Ministry was not an easy task. Quite a number of Air Marshals wanted it for themselves, and I received orders from them to deliver it or to disclose where it was. Using all the tact and delay of which I was capable, I postponed doing either of these things. On the 22nd of August 1945, I said goodbye to all the personnel of the Army Commander's Flight, after I had first done my utmost to arrange for them all to be posted wherever they wished to go. It was another sad farewell. Then I flew our remaining Auster to Northolt where I handed it over to the RAF.

I called on AG6 at the War Office and they allowed me to remain on leave until I was demobilized.

Diana and I rented a flat in London and I resumed civilian life as a barrister. It was lovely for me to be at last living with Diana and our daughter Vivien. But, after the thrills of five years of flying during the War, it was very hard indeed to settle down as a civilian.

General Dempsey wrote to me from Singapore. I valued the last paragraph of his letter so highly that I have kept this letter all these forty years. I will end these Memoirs by setting out a copy of this letter. I should mention that he always called our Austers 'Whizzers'.

HEADQUARTERS,
FOURTEENTH ARMY,
SINGAPORE,
23 September 1945

My Dear Andrew,

Many thanks for your letter of August 25th, which took a long time to reach me.

Thank you so much for dealing with the Storch and the spare parts. You seem to have handled the Air Ministry very diplomatically. No doubt I shall have the usual wrangle with them before it is finally cleared up. This will take a long time as our communications out here are so bad.

As regards Cpl Griffiths and Taylor, I am quite content to leave Griffiths in England, and have told Evy not to send him out. Taylor came with me in the York and has now joined 224 Gp out here.

Oliver has been acting as second pilot in my Dakota for the last month and has now just begun to fly an L5. Distances – such as Kandy to Singapore direct – are a bit long for whizzers!

I came onto Singapore on September 10th and we are now busy getting Malaya into shape. Things are remarkably good and normal life is being resumed very quickly.

I have got a nice little packet of 100,000 Japs concentrated in Johore. They give no trouble whatever and may be said to have joined the Allied Nations.

I don't expect I shall be out here very long myself. When I come back to England I will get in touch with you.

It was a good day when I first met you at Cairon, and I can never sufficiently express my gratitude to you for the splendid way in which you ran your Squadron and my private flying.

Yours ever
M. DEMPSEY

NOTE

I have said that several of my pilots flew passengers into the Russian Zone after the cessation of hostilities. I have now been told by Walter Montagu (our 'Monty') that this was not the case.

One day I was asked to send a pilot to fly a Russian-speaking interpreter to the HQ of General Smirnov who was, I believe, a Russian Army Commander. The interpreter's task was to invite General Smirnov and a number of high-ranking Russian generals to a party that was to be given by our Army Commander at Tac Army. I sent Monty to fly the interpreter there and back.

Monty assumed, as I did, that it would be quite safe for us to fly over the Russian Zone now that all hostilities in Europe had ended. Fortunately he decided to call in and refuel at the airfield of the American 18th Airborne Division at Hagenau before crossing the border between the Eastern and Western Zones. There he was strongly advised not to attempt to fly over the Russian Zone as the Russians habitually shot at our aircraft. The Americans provided an armoured jeep to take him and the interpreter to their destination and back.

Shortly after they had crossed the border they were thoroughly interrogated, after which they were invited to call in there on their return journey and attend a party which was to be held there at about 1600 hrs that day. But Monty wisely decided that a Russian party might render him unfit to fly to Tac Army, and so did not in fact call in as requested.

After that party General Smirnov invited our generals to a party at his HQ, and Monty followed the same procedure as before when taking the interpreter there in order to agree the arrangements. When they were again interrogated after crossing the border, they were asked why they had not come to the party during their previous visit. They were then told that they were very lucky not to have been there as a Russian soldier had got extremely drunk and had sprayed the other guests with the Russian equivalent of the sten gun and there had been a number of casualties.

On this occasion on their way back through the Russian Zone they saw some Russian soldiers burying one of their comrades in a ditch beside the road. They were told that two soldiers had quarrelled over which was to have a certain German girl and one had shot the other.

The Russians treated all German girls as part of the spoils of war. Some years later I was told by the Hungarian girl whom Geoffrey had married after the War of a Russian soldier with a rifle who had stopped a bus in Budapest, ordered every girl on it to take off all her clothes, selected one of these girls for himself and then waved the bus on.

It must have been hell to have been occupied by a Russian Army.